D0093077

FIRE IN MY EYES

FIRE IN MY EYES

AN AMERICAN WARRIOR'S JOURNEY
FROM BEING BLINDED ON THE
BATTLEFIELD TO GOLD MEDAL VICTORY

BRAD SNYDER

AND

TOM SILEO

DA CAPO PRESS

Copyright © 2016 by Brad Snyder and Tom Sileo

Published in the United States by Da Capo Press, an imprint of Perseus Books,
a division of PBG Publishing, LLC, a subsidiary of Hachette Book Group, Inc.

The names of certain US service members have been changed to protect operational
security.

All rights reserved. No part of this publication may be reproduced, stored in a
retrieval system, or transmitted, in any form or by any means, electronic, mechanical,
photocopying, recording, or otherwise, without the prior written permission of
the publisher. Printed in the United States of America. For information, address
Da Capo Press, 44 Farnsworth Street, Third Floor, Boston, MA 02210.

LCCN: 2016014788
ISBN: 978-0-306-82514-9 (hardcover)
ISBN: 978-0-306-82515-6 (e-book)

Published by Da Capo Press
www.dacapopress.com

Da Capo Press books are available at special discounts for bulk purchases in the
U.S. by corporations, institutions, and other organizations. For more information,
please contact the Special Markets Department at 2300 Chestnut Street, Suite 200,
Philadelphia, PA 19103, or call (800) 810-4145, ext. 5000,
or e-mail special.markets@perseusbooks.com.

10 9 8 7 6 5 4 3 2 1

*This book is dedicated to liberty
and to those who serve to protect it.*

CONTENTS

CONTENTS

Shadows of Dawn

Blue hues replaced the black of night as the morning of September 7, 2011, dawned in war-torn southern Afghanistan. No longer needing night vision equipment to reveal what was once obscured in darkness, I removed my helmet and night optical devices (NODs).

Amid the spray-painted camouflage on my helmet was a pronounced "X," reflecting my call sign: "X-ray." This symbol designated me as the expert in explosive hazards for our assault team. Most often, my job as a US Navy Explosive Ordnance Disposal (EOD) officer was to locate or disable improvised explosive devices (IEDs) that have been so prevalently planted by insurgents and terrorists in Afghanistan and Iraq.

In preparation for our impending daylight patrol, I carefully tucked my helmet into a small backpack that I used to carry explosive charges, thermobaric grenades, and other tools of the trade. I found my ball cap and pulled it down over my mess of long, reddish-blonde hair. I zipped up my pack and slung each of my arms through its shoulder straps, tugging them until the pack fit snugly across my body armor.

From a crouched position atop the roof of a two-story, mud-walled building, I gazed across the fertile grape fields in the southernmost valley of Kandahar. Other members of my commando unit, made up of US Navy SEALs and Afghan Special Forces, were in a small courtyard below my watch position.

Through the shadows of dawn, I carefully studied everything between me and the horizon, looking for anything that might pose a hazard to me or my unit. As I scanned westward from the sun peering over the horizon in the east sky, I could trace the outline of a mountain range against the still-starry sky. The most prominent peak was directly north of me, with its sharp rock outcroppings turning a reddish orange as rays of sunlight penetrated my field of view. The shadows then began to extend from the base of the rock outcroppings into a barren red sand desert to my west and south. The picturesque circles of sand dunes etched into the terrain by the wind were in stark contrast to the jagged rocks to my north.

My gaze drifted back east, following the luscious vineyards in the mountain valley surrounding me. I tilted my head back and looked at the sky, which now presented a gorgeous array of purple, blue, red, and orange. The brushstrokes of vibrant color were glittered with the fading stars of the night sky. For a very brief moment, I released the pistol grip of the M4 automatic rifle slung across my chest and soaked in my rooftop view. In that rare moment, it occurred to me that I was looking at one of the most beautiful things I had ever seen.

At the same time, it saddened me to think that the magnificence of this faraway land was juxtaposed with the evil of its Taliban oppressors, who had a grip on the very village I was observing. My heart ached for the families that had suffered the loss of loved ones or had been forced to leave their homes. It saddened me even more to know that these charming grape fields were filled with hundreds of large, devastating IEDs, all capable of snatching the lives of those unlucky enough to step on them.

For a fleeting moment, the warmth of the rising sun was enough to wash away these thoughts. Once again, I swept my gaze from the east across the mountain range, desert dunes, grape fields, and the morning sky above the sleepy Afghan village. I was in complete awe of the majesty of the sights before me.

It was the last sunrise I would ever see.

1

The Monsters of Weeki Wachee Springs

From the edge of a small platform, suspended in the middle of a clear, dark lake, my five-year-old eyes gazed into the chilly water. My parents and grandparents had brought me to beautiful Weeki Wachee, near my grandparents' house in my home state of Florida. As legend would have it, mermaids swim among the caves formed by the Weeki Wachee Springs.

As a five-year-old child, I had a strong belief in this myth. To further this vision, my father, Michael Snyder, pointed out a large, white conch shell at the bottom, and what appeared to be strands of mermaid hair—which was actually seaweed—entangling it. Fascinated, I told my dad that I wanted to investigate the shell. He nodded in encouragement, and watched me don a small mask as I entered the water.

Once immersed, I looked toward the shell, which was seemingly hundreds of feet below. In reality, the shell was only twenty feet down.

I took a deep breath and kicked my legs over my head to descend. I kicked, stroked, and then kicked again. The burning in my lungs grew, and the water's pressure pushed on my ears and mask in a way I had never felt before.

A few feet down, I began to imagine monsters that might be lurking in the dark waters around me. Jules Verne-style giant squid swam alongside freakishly large great white sharks in the depths of my imagination, and I began to panic. I aborted my mission and shot up to the surface.

I panted heavily as I searched around for my dad, who, I finally noticed, was watching intently from a nearby swimming platform. I began giving him an elaborate description of the scary seascape that I imagined. Without being able to fully understand my garbled words, my dad recognized my fear and jumped into the water next to me. He grabbed me by the shoulders while treading water and explained that while I might be afraid, the only way to conquer my fears was to acknowledge and embrace them. He asked if I was willing to give up on the wonders of the deep, the shell, and the mermaid's hair because I was afraid.

"I'm not afraid!" I exclaimed with all the bravado that a five-year-old could muster, even though I was.

My dad smiled and said that he would go down there with me.

Together, we spit in our masks like Richard Dreyfuss in *Jaws*. After wiping the masks clean and putting them on, we took deep breaths and kicked our feet over our heads. We descended toward the imaginary sea monsters.

Once again, I became afraid as I kicked and stroked. Sensing my fright, my dad put a hand on my shoulder and ushered me further down. I looked at his face, which was oddly squished because of his mask, and saw him nod in encouragement. My dad's presence and support steeled my youthful resolve, and I began furiously stroking towards the conch shell.

As the burning and pressure intensified, I finally reached the white shell. I planted my little feet on the sandy bottom, grabbed a hold of the shell, and pushed off with all of the energy that I had left.

After kicking furiously, I returned to the surface in triumph. While gasping for air, I placed the shell and mermaid hair—as I firmly believed it was—on the swimming platform.

As always, my dad was right there to congratulate me. Together, we investigated the bounty I had stolen from the monsters of Weeki Wachee Springs.

MY FATHER AND MY MOTHER, Valarie, met while they were teammates on a medical emergency response team in Reno, Nevada. My mom was a neonatal intensive care nurse, while my dad was a respiratory therapist. Together, they would board a small helicopter and fly to remote parts of Nevada to pick up sick or premature newborns, and bring them back to the better-equipped hospital in Reno.

After I was born, we moved to Florida to be closer to my grandparents. Before long, our family began expanding, first with my brother, Mitch, and then my youngest brother, Russ. In the hopes of eventually earning more money, my dad began taking night classes in electrical engineering, while my mom began picking up every possible overtime nursing shift.

To make things a little easier on my mother, her dad would often take me off her hands for a weekend, or even a full week. I absolutely loved these adventures with my grandpa. He lived about eight miles from Weeki Wachee Springs in Brooksville, Florida.

My grandpa, Forrest Lindsey, literally laid the foundation for his retirement by buying a plot of land and building Lindsey Acres, a small neighborhood subdivision. On the largest lot, he designed and built his dream home, where he and my grandma would enjoy their retirement. Even at the age of five, I knew I wanted to be just like my grandpa.

As I grew up and started going through old photos, I learned that my grandpa had served in the Navy. My grandma would later explain he had been a torpedo man during World War II. Incredibly, my grandfather's honorable service in the Pacific had included the epic Battle of Midway, which famously took place six months after the Japanese attacked Pearl Harbor.

Following his tours of duty, my grandpa returned to the East Coast to train new recruits. Then, his airplane crashed off the coast of New York, killing everyone aboard except for my grandpa, who would spend four years recovering from severe injuries. It was then that he fell in love with his nurse: my grandma.

After hearing my grandma's story, I saw my grandpa in a whole new light. I couldn't believe he had lived such an impressive life without feeling the need to speak about his enormous accomplishments. After I finally recognized his humility, courage, and unconditional love, my grandfather instantly became my hero. I could only hope to live a life worthy of his example.

ABOUT A YEAR LATER, my dad and I were attending an air show at Peterson Air Force Base in Colorado Springs, Colorado. Seeking new work opportunities and a cheaper cost of living, my family had relocated there when I was six years old.

In amazement, I stared up at a small aircraft deftly maneuvering across the pale blue sky, as its daredevil antics left behind trails of white smoke. After an intricate series of barrel rolls, steep climbs, and terrifying dives, the aircraft disappeared from view. In the silence left behind by the departing aircraft, I surveyed the airstrip in front of me.

I glanced up at my father, who was standing to my left, and I noticed him dialing his binoculars toward a spot on the runway near the horizon. Following his gaze, I noticed the profile of a dark, ominous-looking aircraft that seemed to be constructed from many flat panels glued together into a strange, yet elegantly symmetrical and cohesive triangular shape. My dad then knelt down and explained that the craft was an F-117 stealth fighter, designed by the US military to creep under the radar systems of our enemies to spy and sometimes attack the bad guys.

My dad was always passionate about learning, reading, and understanding the way things worked, but there was a special respect exuded whenever he spoke about the military. We would spend hours playing catch outside while he told stories, including the exploits of his father, Vincent Snyder, who after serving in World War II, spent the rest of his life building US Navy ships that would carry future generations of sailors and Marines. As we tossed the ball back and forth, my dad explained how brave American warriors prevented evil dictators from threatening our way of life.

Always inspired by my father's lessons, I would then go straight from playing catch to leading my G.I. Joe heroes—Duke, Sgt. Slaughter, and Snake Eyes—in ferocious combat assaults on our backyard's small sand dunes. I would continue playing with G.I. Joes throughout my childhood, and like so many young American boys, dream of becoming a real-life warrior.

Sometimes, after the sinking sun brought us inside, I was allowed the special privilege of staying up late. My younger brothers and my newborn baby sister, Elyse, were put to bed while my father and I settled in for our favorite show, *Tour of Duty*, which was about an infantry platoon during the Vietnam War. Seated on the floor, my little feet tapped along to the beat of "Paint It Black" by The Rolling Stones as images of jungles, helicopters, and American soldiers flashed across the screen. My dad always sat behind me, rocking gently in his bentwood rocker, and answered my many questions about the show and our country's military.

Occasionally, when my mom worked the night shift at the hospital, my dad and I would venture to the video store and pick out a war movie that we hadn't seen. Our mutual favorite was *Platoon*. Over the years, we'd watch everything from *Apocalypse Now* to *Stripes*.

I didn't realize it until much later in life, but my desire to serve came from these early experiences. I could hear my father's deep-rooted respect for our armed services in his many lessons and stories as we stood outside playing catch. His own inner child was exposed whenever we went to air shows or when he'd let me stay up late with him to watch war movies. He always had a gleam in his eye when he spoke about his own dad, and I remember wanting to earn that same respect. I wanted to make my dad proud, and I wanted him to talk about me with that same gleam in his eye.

OUR TIME IN THE Colorado mountains didn't last long. Struggling with the demands of four young kids and missing the warmth of the beach, my family returned to Florida when I was nine years old. I was a pretty awkward kid, and starting over in a new school wasn't easy, but I was glad to be closer to my hero, Grandpa Lindsey, who we saw every few weekends. Sadly, though, Grandpa died of cancer less than three years later, leaving behind an incredible legacy and a family who loved him very much.

MY FATHER DROVE ME to the local pool to try out for the swim team when I was eleven years old. While my early dive into Weeki Wachee Springs had given me an appreciation for the water and confidence in my swimming ability, those feelings largely disappeared when I witnessed the swim team's practice. These young athletes swam with great elegance and precision, and I doubted that I could ever reach their level.

After testing my raw, unpolished skills, the team's tough and burly coach, Todd Mann, surprisingly told my dad that while I "needed work," I could start practicing with the team the very next day.

My first practices were horrible, and I repeatedly voiced my frustrations to my dad. In response, he would tell me that nothing worth doing ever came easily. He said that if I truly dedicated myself, I would achieve success, and that the feeling of accomplishment after so much hard work would make the endeavor worthwhile.

I heeded my dad's advice and resolved to work as hard as I could every day, even as other kids teased me for looking like a dork in my new Speedo swimsuit. Before long, I started making progress. Striving to continually improve then became almost addictive in nature.

A few summers later, I was well-trained, polished, and much stronger. I remember feeling elated while taking my first lead in a big race, only to feel crushed after realizing that I had lost by a few hundredths of a second.

After drying off, I looked up at my father expecting to see disappointment. To my surprise, he was sporting a huge grin.

"Great job, Brad," he shouted in excitement. "That's your best time ever by over forty-five seconds!"

I couldn't believe it. How could my dad be so dim? He had completely glossed over the fact that despite all the effort, I had come up short. I lost! How could he not see that?

My father truly didn't care whether I won or not. Whenever I struggled in the pool or in life, my dad would explain that each failure reveals an opportunity to make ourselves better. He taught me not to define my success by results, but by the virtue attained in the process. Even though I lost that race, my dad's lesson erased any remaining doubts about whether I could compete and eventually succeed. From that day forward, I wanted to be a swimmer.

MY EARLY RESOLUTIONS TO swim and to serve were never written down. I didn't discuss them with anyone, and honestly didn't even think about these dreams or realize that they had become an integral part of my character. That was, until I was introduced to the United States Naval Academy.

I was offered a tour of Annapolis, Maryland, during my sophomore year of high school, and was instantly enamored with the legendary institution. With my eyes wide open and mouth agape, we strolled down Stribling Walk, paid homage to Tecumseh and John Paul Jones, and met a few midshipmen who greeted us with enthusiasm. The gravity of Navy's Bancroft Hall sucked me in, and I knew with one hundred percent certainty that Annapolis was where I wanted to begin my adult life.

Before leaving town, I stopped by the Admissions Office and inquired about starting the painstaking process of becoming a midshipman. I was handed a small checklist of items and targets for aspiring candidates. That checklist may as well have been a religious text, as I studied and committed to its every letter for the rest of my high school years.

2

To Lead and to Serve

I was a seventeen-year-old high school senior in St. Petersburg, Florida, on September 11, 2001. That morning, my classmates and I were in hysterics as we discussed the jokes and innuendos of Aeschylus's tragedies in AP English. We had all thoroughly enjoyed this class due to Mrs. Archer, a teacher with a keen ability to generate compelling dialogue about classic literature.

At about 9:00 a.m., another teacher darted into the room with a very sullen look on her face. Without even acknowledging that students were present, she whispered something into Mrs. Archer's ear. Our teacher's head bowed as she hurriedly turned on the television. The class fell quiet.

The screen was immediately filled with horrifying, confusing images of thick black smoke pouring out of one of the Twin Towers. After a few very puzzling moments, we collectively gasped as we watched a large passenger jet fly into the World Trade Center tower on the right side of the screen.

The world seemed to stand still as we hung on every word of the news anchors, who seemed just as astonished as we were. They then told us about plane crashes at the Pentagon and a Pennsylvania field. We watched in dismay as the Twin Towers collapsed in giant clouds of thick, gray dust.

For the rest of the day, the normal sounds of high school kids gossiping and slamming lockers were replaced with deafening silence. The fact that our collective freedom—and lives, for that matter—had just been gravely threatened was not lost on my group of friends. Even as teenagers, our hearts ached for the victims of this horrendous terrorist attack. I also remember returning home to blankly stare at the TV screen with my mom, dad, and siblings.

When I had woken up that fateful Tuesday morning, my dreams revolved around attending the Naval Academy, competing as a Division I swimmer, and becoming a Navy officer. When I went to bed on the night of September 11, 2001, those dreams were replaced with a strong determination to serve our country in whatever capacity I could.

I resolved that night that, even if my plans to attend the Naval Academy fell through, I would enlist in the Navy anyway. I wanted to dedicate my life to a cause that would prevent evil men like Osama bin Laden from attacking our homeland.

AS US TROOPS FOUGHT al Qaeda and the Taliban in Afghanistan on December 22, 2001, I was returning from an exhausting high school swim practice in Florida. When I got home, I was greeted by a thin FedEx envelope postmarked from Maryland.

My hands trembled as I ripped open the envelope to find a single leaf of high-quality letterhead, emblazoned with the Naval Academy's crest. Across the page was a detailed memorandum, but my seventeen-year-old eyes moved directly to six words that would forever change my life: "Welcome to the Class of 2006!"

A few weeks later, another package would arrive from the same Annapolis address. It contained strict guidance for the Navy's "Induction Day," or "I-Day" as it is more commonly known. The packet stressed the physical rigors I would endure during my "plebe summer," which all new midshipmen are required to participate in before the fall semester, including push-ups, sit-ups, and long runs in the summer heat. A significant number of incoming freshmen, or "plebes" as they are called at the Naval Academy, would drop out after being exposed to plebe summer's rigors.

Every day for three months, I worked out even harder than I was already training as a swimmer. I felt physically ready for plebe summer after those ninety days, but as I prepared to leave everything I knew and loved in St. Petersburg, I began to wonder if I was mentally prepared for Annapolis.

I read all available literature on what to expect from plebe summer. I asked anyone and everyone for their advice. Out of all the help that I received, my father's words stood out, as always.

"Be honest and be yourself," he said. "Be quiet and humble unless called upon. Be determined, motivated, and always on your guard. Don't let them see you suffer."

That valuable advice was similar to what my dad had been saying as we worked toward success in the pool. Because I had been swimming since age eleven, I knew that I could push myself beyond perceived physical limits, while also accomplishing my goals with a strong mind. I hoped that things would be the same during plebe summer, but no matter how hard I tried to block out negative thoughts, uncertainty and doubt still loomed.

EACH "I-DAY" CANDIDATE WAS allowed to bring a small backpack containing a baseball glove and a tennis racket. As my father and I rummaged through our small Florida garage for the necessary items, I zeroed in on the Pee Wee Mag baseball glove that I had been using since I was six. The glove was tattered and no longer fit, but it was the only mitt I ever used during those backyard catches when my dad taught me what it meant to be an American.

As I loaded up my goods, my father noticed the wear and tear on my childhood glove and proceeded to dig around for his own. He insisted that I bring his glove to the Naval Academy instead. Deeply honored, I jammed the glove into my backpack.

I cherished my father's gift. It comforted me that I was bringing a piece of his life with me into the unknown dangers of the post-9/11 world. I knew that when I looked at the glove in Annapolis and wherever I'd go next—maybe even a battlefield—that I would be able to hear my dad's comforting words of encouragement. I would also remember our backyard catches, and that yearning desire I would always feel to make him proud.

3

Annapolis

I arrived in Annapolis on the night before I-Day. The evening was uneventful except for my visit to a Marine supply depot. I bought a small American flag, which would hang in my room for the next four-plus years. Even in the toughest moments, I knew the flag would always remind me what I was studying and training for.

After being awakened at 0500 the next morning by the clanging of metal and shouts of upperclassmen, I-Day officially began at 0900. As I stood in a large arena without knowing what to expect, my first task was to simply state my name and present a form of identification. I smiled at an attractive blonde woman as I showed her my Florida driver's license.

She was unmoved by my gesture of friendliness. Instead, the woman curtly instructed me to memorize six digits: 066420. Those digits were now my "alpha code," or identifier. In the eyes of my new Naval Academy superiors, I was no longer Brad Snyder from St. Petersburg. I was 066420.

While half of me felt like a prison inmate, the other half was thrilled. I couldn't have been more proud or excited. Upon realizing that I really was doing this—becoming part of the US Naval Academy community—I couldn't help but crack a smile.

My grin was met with dirty looks from the "cadre," or Naval Academy detailers who barked orders and got us ready to be midshipmen. They yelled at me to stop looking around, stand at attention, and to wipe that stupid smirk off my face. Not wishing to call any more attention to myself, I took my place in line and intently stared at the back of the head in front of me.

We were then shepherded into a makeshift barbershop, where our hair—and perhaps the last remaining aspect of our individuality—was shaved off.

I was then presented with a small blue book that had *Reef Points* emblazoned on the front in gold lettering. All of us were matter-of-factly told to memorize the book, which was filled with Navy trivia and quotes from the likes of John Paul Jones and Teddy Roosevelt, cover to cover. The thought of memorizing every word seemed daunting, if not impossible.

During the rest of I-Day, various cadre members would invade my personal space and demand that I recite a *Reef Points* passage. The book had only been in my pocket for a few minutes, so how the heck was I supposed to have this stuff memorized already? The red-faced cadre members showed no sympathy, and berated me each time I responded with "I don't know." In addition to Reef Points, I would also be required to memorize the only five basic responses I would be allowed to direct at a member of the cadre. "I don't know" was not one of them.

The next morning, we were required to swarm into a hallway at 0500 on the dot and scream "Go Navy!" or "Beat Army!" every time we moved a muscle. We then began the process of learning how to march in formation.

"066420!" one cadre shouted in my ear at 0503. "Do you know what time it is?!?"

We were not allowed to wear wristwatches, yet we were, of course, expected to be perfectly punctual. After only three minutes of my first full day as a midshipman, I was rapidly learning that the next four-plus years would be full of orders, even if they were completely illogical. My duty was not to question the demands of my superiors, but to do what I was told. In order to become a leader, you must first learn to be a follower.

"Sir, I'll find out what time it is and report back, sir!" I said, probably sounding ridiculous.

Games like these filled each day of plebe summer. In between sessions of basic seamanship, leadership, swimming, and marching, we would time how fast we could change uniforms. We timed how fast we could make and remake our beds. We even timed how fast we could shower, even though we usually began sweating like pigs almost immediately after the competition.

As the summer wore on, however, we began to wear our sweaty stench with pride. We gelled as a group, learning how to help one another. Instead of becoming flustered, frustrated, or otherwise upset when we were yelled at, my class began to understand these games for what they were: a much-needed introduction to military life. With our country at war, it was even more important to quickly learn these urgent lessons.

As I developed mentally, my physical state suffered slightly. In high school, I had struggled to keep weight on. I was swimming at least two and a half hours a day; sometimes up to six or seven miles. I was probably burning up to 8,000 calories per day. During plebe summer, however, I was consuming the same number of calories per day at the dining hall without burning off nearly as much. During the six-week period of plebe summer, I gained 14 pounds.

I felt terrible in the water after gaining so much weight. I was also concerned about whether I would be able to swim competitively at the Division I level. As my plebe summer ended and my first swimming season at Navy got underway, I struggled badly in my opening meet. The poor results in successive competitions prompted me to train even harder, which began to negatively affect my grades.

I had never needed to work very hard in high school, but the academic workload of a Naval Academy midshipman is a completely different story. For the first time, I struggled to learn new material. I did not have my dad around to explain the complex math involved in college-level engineering courses, and my photographic memory became overloaded due to the sheer volume of information. I rarely even got a "B" in high school, so the sight of my first "F" at Navy was startling. I soon fell behind, and the prospect of being tossed out of the Academy terrified me.

Another huge challenge was the fact that I woke up at 0430 each morning for swim practice. Almost every night, I would return to my room in a worn-down, exhausted state. With my alarm clock always set for 0430 the following day, the last thing I usually felt like doing was cracking open a book.

While the punishing training regimen had a hugely negative impact on my grades, it finally began to pay off in the pool. When I won my first Division I event against Army—our fiercest rival—I heard my dad's words of encouragement inside my head as I made my final kicks and touched the wall in triumph.

As we celebrated beating Army in that big meet, I finally felt like I belonged at the Naval Academy. Not only did I get to wear a uniform that said "Navy" on the front, but I had driven myself to be part of something bigger than myself.

4

The Dark Ages

At the Naval Academy, the beginning of January through the onset of spring is often referred to as "the dark ages." It's generally a depressing time for midshipmen, as the Maryland weather is often cold and icy, with no Navy football games to look forward to on weekends. Like the snow that would sometimes gather on brittle tree limbs, the burden of our rigorous schedules always seemed to feel heaviest during this gloomy period.

The third quarter of my junior year in Annapolis represented my personal dark ages. I was inundated with schoolwork, which was even more difficult due to my poor study habits. Even though I was surrounded by teammates and friends, I felt alone in my struggles, as everyone else seemed to manage the load with relative ease. I also found myself highly frustrated by my lack of improvement in the pool. No matter how much of an extra effort I made, it didn't seem to be making the slightest bit of difference.

My motivation began to slip once I started being left out of the Navy swim team's starting lineup. If I wasn't even swimming in meets, I started to wonder why I was working so hard to maintain mediocrity. With my grades suffering, I thought, maybe I could better utilize the six-plus hours a day I was devoting to training?

I began to succumb to cynicism and doubt. From age eleven until my junior year at Navy, I had rarely, if ever, missed a swimming practice. That included bouts with ear infections, the flu, and even a broken wrist. The only time I could remember missing practice was when my dad punished me for cheating on a Spanish quiz during my freshman year of high school. He said that swimming was a privilege, which I had voided by compromising my integrity. Sitting out of practice that day was horrible, and taught me a valuable lesson.

Despite my previously unwavering work ethic, however, I started hitting the snooze button when the alarm went off for morning practice. I also started skipping classes. The result of my laziness was being summoned to the office of my swimming coach, and before long, to the Commandant of the Naval Academy, who was a much more intimidating equivalent of a university dean.

My punishment was being assigned to "restriction," which meant I couldn't leave campus. Due to another aspect of my punishment, "tours," I was also required to march a square pattern in a courtyard for one hour per day. Both assignments were miserable, and offered plenty of time for serious reflection.

I started to wonder how I had gotten myself into this situation. Even as a junior, I began to question if I was qualified to be a midshipman, let alone lead US Navy sailors during wartime, should I be lucky enough to graduate. Just like the butterflies that often fluttered in my stomach before a big race, skeptical thoughts were now swimming through my head.

MEMORIAL HALL—LOCATED IN THE heart of the Naval Academy's historic Bancroft Hall—is a museum that honors fallen midshipmen and chronicles the Marine Corps' and Navy's rich histories of selfless service. One of the most treasured artifacts inside Memorial Hall is Oliver Hazard Perry's battle flag from the War of 1812, which famously reads, "don't give up the ship!" Another highlight features the heroic exploits of John Ripley, the US Marine officer who almost singlehandedly prevented the North Vietnamese army from capturing Saigon in 1972.

Memorial Hall was also where restriction formations were held. I have almost no doubt that this was intentional, and designed to ensure that troublemakers, like the lazy, junior year version of Brad Snyder, would appreciate the extraordinary responsibilities that came with being a midshipman.

In my case, it absolutely worked. I stared at the miniature version of Ripley and pictured myself leading men in combat. The image of Perry's battle flag, as well as "don't give up the ship," was burned into my memory. For the first time, I began to reimagine myself as a future naval leader.

The warmer weather and blooming flowers of another beautiful Maryland spring enhanced my renewed sense of purpose. I also reached a previously unimaginable conclusion: my military career would be better off if I opted against pursuing a roster spot on the swim team for my next, final year at the Naval Academy. By quitting the swim team, I believed, I would have a much better chance of improving my grades and eventually joining a Special Operations unit.

Then, something happened that I never saw coming. My swimming teammates elected me as their captain. I was blown away and also felt undeserving, especially since I had been planning to quit.

After the shocking announcement, I looked around the room at the fine young men I had been swimming alongside for the past three years. They had chosen me as their leader, and I couldn't let them down. In fact, I never told anyone about my initial decision to quit. Instead, I chose to embrace the honor that my teammates had bestowed on me. As a senior captain, I would set an example and inspire the Naval Academy's swim team in the same way I hoped to someday lead our country's bravest men and women into battle.

TWO OF THE PREVIOUS three Naval Academy men's swim team captains had gone straight into the Navy's Basic Underwater Demolition/SEAL (BUD/S) training upon graduation. The third, my best friend Jake, had just earned a selection into the Explosive Ordnance Disposal community, which was where I hoped to end up. All three were warriors who inspired me deeply, which meant that I had big shoes to fill as the new team captain. But I still didn't feel worthy to succeed these fine young men, especially after my lousy junior season. On top of it all, I was afraid of public speaking. At the time, I could imagine nothing more terrifying than delivering locker room speeches before each meet.

Then, I thought about how my dad reacted after I lost that big race when I was eleven. It didn't matter if I had won or lost, but that I had left everything in the pool. I thought about Perry's "don't give up the ship" flag and Ripley's extraordinary valor while staring down the North Vietnamese Army. I decided that I would embrace my new role as captain, and—through my work ethic—inspire my teammates to succeed.

When it came time to deliver my first address as the new team captain, my fidgety hands were both cold and sweaty. That was until my eyes circled the room and showed me the faces of forty young men who believed in me. Most importantly, they believed in our team, as well as themselves. That's when I realized that it didn't really matter what I said, as long as I exuded confidence.

As I began to speak, I did so from the heart instead of the prepared remarks I had been practicing in my head. My teammates nodded as I spoke, and I knew that they were ready to follow me into the water. As was our tradition, we strode confidently onto the pool deck, huddled together, and joined the home crowd in a huge pre-race cheer.

I wish I could remember whether we won or lost that meet. But as my father had taught me when I was eleven, it didn't matter. Through my experiences as the captain of that group of young men, I had learned two of the most valuable leadership lessons of my career.

First, leadership is living a positive example, day in and day out. Second, compassion should be the basis for all leadership. If you can live the positive example, and wholly invest yourself in the people around you while demonstrating true compassion, then you will be able to establish an unfaltering trust. People will then follow you anywhere.

Shortly after our final swim meet during my last year in Annapolis, I sat in the locker room after everyone else had left. I took a few minutes to consider the end of my swimming career, and how in the water I had grown from a small boy into a soon-to-be naval officer. While I was sad to leave the sport, I was simultaneously thrilled to begin a new career in the Navy.

After four years buried in textbooks and spreadsheets, I would also find that the lessons I learned on the pool deck were among the most valuable that I learned at the Naval Academy. Finally, I was ready to lead.

5

Two Left Shoes

A gentle yet incessant tapping sound echoed down a long hallway. The hour was late, and the occupancy of the historic Naval Academy building had been reduced to a mere handful.

The tapping was being caused by the shoe on my left foot, which nervously bounced as I stared at a large, wooden door sealing off a classroom that normally bustled with crowds of uniform-clad midshipmen.

Behind that door was a small room with a large table where three steel-faced US Navy officers were sitting. At the end of each sleeve of their black suit jackets were multiple rings of gold, indicating many years of honorable service. On the left side of their chests were colorful ribbons that told stories of heroism across the globe. Just above this storied grid sat a gold pin in the shape of a wreath.

Among the pin's features were a bomb, lightning bolts, and a gold star. As I had learned during my studies, the bomb represents the mission of the EOD community, which is to render safe all explosive hazards that can kill or maim American troops and innocent civilians. The crossed lightning bolts represent both the bomb's lethal power and the courage of those who disable it.

The star represents the highest level of EOD achievement. Each of the three men at the table wore one, which meant they were EOD officers and, by definition, leaders.

On the large table in front of each officer was a tall stack of neatly organized packets. Each piece of paper helped tell the life story of the fifty or so midshipmen vying to follow in their footsteps. With firm expressions and clenched jaws, these three American warriors would decide the future of the midshipman seated at the opposite end of the table.

Back then, it was often said that the EOD community was the best-kept secret in the Navy. The small group consisted of the smartest, most capable sailors, and these sailors were required to maintain a diverse skill set including SCUBA diving, jumping out of airplanes, and blowing things up. I had learned this wonderful secret from EOD officers while training in Panama City, Florida, during midshipman dive training.

I was quickly enamored by these special men and women. Admittedly, I also loved the idea of growing my hair long and spending the bulk of my time diving off the shores of my home state's beautiful Gulf Coast. Of course, as I would come to find out, diving is only a small portion of the EOD training regimen. But the more I learned, the more I wanted to become a part of this amazing group.

The Navy EOD community requires an additional level of screening. Physical, mental, and moral evaluations are all incorporated in the process, which is both lengthy and nerve-wracking for those who apply. Generally, there are only a dozen places available for new EOD officers. About forty to sixty kids annually seek one of these coveted spots.

After a very long forty-five minutes of waiting for my good friend Trip to finish his evaluation, the door finally swung open. As our eyes locked, he immediately shook his head.

"I don't know, man," Trip said in apparent defeat, which was completely out of character for my burly fellow midshipman. "It's tough in there."

My small amount of confidence rapidly vanished as I slumped into my seat. My left foot was tapping more nervously than ever.

About fifteen minutes later, I settled into my chair in front of the three respected, imposing EOD officers. They began flipping through my life story, and one by one, asking questions. To my initial relief, they were largely softballs that I was able to field with confidence. That was until the toughest question, which thankfully, I had been preparing to answer not only out in the hallway, but for many preceding weeks.

"Midshipman Snyder, it's no secret that your grades are less than stellar and don't stack up well against your classmates'," one of the officers bluntly began. "Can you justify why we might consider selecting a candidate with such a low grade point average and overall class standing?"

The reality of this question was harsh, but also completely fair. I knew I had to account for my poor performance, while also giving the board confidence that despite my academic struggles in Annapolis, I would not fail out of EOD School in Fort Walton Beach, Florida.

I admitted that my low grades were due to bad time management. I also conceded that I had placed a larger priority on athletics, and never quite managed to adapt to the historically rigorous academic structure of US service academy life.

At the same time, I pointed out that my grades had been steadily improving over the past few semesters. In conclusion, I explained that I hadn't come to the Naval Academy to become an architect, but a military officer who wanted to lead troops in combat. EOD School was the next logical step, and an opportunity that I would embrace. Simply put, I would not allow myself to fail.

All three men nodded thoughtfully as they considered my reply. I was then asked to prove my aptitude by drawing out and explaining a complicated aspect of ship design. I was extremely nervous while making my presentation, but thankfully, the officers were once again nodding when I was finished.

It was then that one the three EOD officers—a captain—began a lengthy, motivating soliloquy about my leadership development and how I would best serve the EOD community and its elite sailors. He said things like, "when you get to EOD School . . ." and "when you check in to your first unit . . ." Since he was speaking in such definitive terms, it seemed as though I had been selected. I must have performed favorably.

After shaking each officer's hand, the sound of my dress shoes tapping on the marble floor once again filled that long, daunting Naval Academy hallway. This time, however, those taps didn't signify nervousness, but pure elation. My dream of becoming an EOD officer candidate was about to come true.

UPON GRADUATING FROM THE Naval Academy in 2006 and subsequently receiving my invitation to join the storied EOD community, I received orders to return to Dive School—where I had spent one summer as a midshipman—in Panama City. Dive School was the first step in the nearly eighteen-month training pipeline created to prepare new selectees for the demands of being an EOD operator. I was now a US Navy ensign, and even though I was already SCUBA qualified, I was excited to get a chance to refine my diving skills.

I opted to all but shave my head for the beginning of Dive School. I wanted to set a positive example for my peers, and a sharp, clean appearance is always a smart way to make a good first impression. I took my time to ensure a close, thorough shave, as missed spots not only look bad, but might be grounds to fail my first inspection. My summer white uniform had also been meticulously prepared. I even bought a shiny, brand-new pair of shoes that would hopefully impress my new instructors.

As I opened the shoebox and pulled away the tissue paper, my jaw dropped upon realizing that the box contained two shoes that were both perfect fits . . . for my left foot.

My stomach leapt into my throat. How did I screw this up? Quickly, though, I concluded that there was absolutely nothing I could do about this ridiculous situation. I had to simply roll with it. I randomly selected a shoe and slipped it onto my left foot, before awkwardly jamming the other onto my right, while again berating myself for ending up in such a hilariously desperate situation.

Appropriately, my new classmates found a great deal of humor in my first-day calamity. I vividly remember the commands to march—"left, left, right!"—while the entire class collectively chuckled.

I positioned myself in the middle of our new line and fell into the best possible position for inspection. As I stared ahead blankly, I was mentally preparing for the epic chew-out from one of the already pissed-off instructors that would surely ensue.

A short but menacing-looking chief petty officer's gaze then drifted across my face before moving down to my insignia and ribbons. Finally, his eyes squinted as they settled on my two left shoes.

After a moment of sheer anxiety, I stole a glance at his puzzled face. He stared down in intense contemplation before looking back up at me, and then down again. While he made abundantly clear that he had discovered something awry, it was as if he couldn't quite put his finger on it. He looked up and down a few more times before finally shouting in my ear.

"Are those new shoes, Ensign?" he said.

"Yes, Chief!" I shouted in reply.

After a pause, he offered a curt but surprisingly humorous response.

"Good for you," he said.

All at once, my new band of brothers lost their collective composure. Everyone laughed, and I breathed a huge sigh of relief. Even though I had completely botched my first moments as an EOD officer candidate, I knew that I was in the right place.

6

Hooyah America

Standing next to me in formation during the infamous "two left shoes" incident had been Tyler Trahan. At that point in time, he was a seaman apprentice fresh out of US Navy boot camp, while I was the aforementioned, green-as-can-be ensign straight out of the Academy.

It didn't take long for everyone to admire Tyler and for us to become good friends. Before we even knew each other's names, Tyler was cracking jokes and gently ribbing his classmates. He was sharp and rarely screwed up, often picking up the slack for his lesser-talented classmates. This frequently prevented our class from being punished for silly infractions. No matter how hard we tried, though, we would almost always find ourselves knocking out push-ups after violating some obscure rule. Tyler seemed to have an endless reserve available for such exertions, however, and was able to call out military work songs—or cadence—for the class without betraying an ounce of fatigue.

Soon after initial examinations, Tyler proved himself to be a consistent, top performer. As the junior man, he was often singled out by the instructors and called upon to sing cadence as we ran mile after mile in the Florida heat. We would all make attempts to relieve

Tyler on the outside of the running formation, but no one could do it as well as him. I jumped out on occasion, and would attempt to freestyle different cadences to make the class laugh.

The instructors didn't find me funny, and I was usually shut down quickly, replaced by the rock solid ballads of Tyler Trahan. Due to his booming voice and his innate ability to quickly learn and identify approaching instructors, Tyler became our "hooyah man," assigned to utter a booming "HOOYAH!" as we moved through the daily training exercises.

Every morning at 0800, the national anthem was played over loudspeakers across the base while the flag was hoisted. No matter what we were doing, every trainee was required to drop everything, come to attention, and render honors to our flag. At the conclusion of the anthem, with the flag happily flapping at the top of its mast, it would be the hooyah man's responsibility to call out a "HOOYAH!" to our beloved country. Upon hearing this call, our class would reply in unison with a loud and bellowing "HOOYAH AMERICA!" This is one of my fondest memories of Dive School.

ON A FRIDAY MORNING, after six weeks in Panama City, our class completed the Dive School portion of our training. The following Monday morning, EOD School would start at Fort Eglin Air Force Base, which was about an hour's drive to the west.

While we had been required to live on base during Dive School, we were allowed to live outside the base during EOD School, so I decided to split rent with a few of the other officers in my class. The four of us moved into a large house adjacent to a golf course, located a short drive from the schoolhouse. One of my roommates was my good friend Rex, and the other two, Pete and Slider, would also become dear friends.

That Friday night, in a house that was empty except for four mattresses on the floor, we had a party to celebrate our accomplishments. This was largely instigated by Tyler, who showed up just before sundown with half our class in tow, and a pickup truck that held a quantity of beer that would make any frat boy or sorority sister proud.

Wasting no time, Tyler scrounged together a beer pong table out of scrap wood that had been left in our garage, and immediately started trash talking. Rex and I squared off against Tyler and Pete, and instantly, Rex and I were outmatched. Tyler, of course, was a natural, while Pete had four years at Vanderbilt under his belt. Admittedly, one of the shortcomings of a Naval Academy education is lack of beer pong experience.

Tyler excitedly chanted, "Nuke it!" or "takin' out the trash!" as he and Pete sank ball after ball, while Rex and I threw up one air ball after another. As the night progressed and the number of beers left in the cooler shrank, our fellow partiers either made their respective ways home or found a quiet corner of the house to pass out in. I am certain that Tyler was the last to give up and turn in that night, though, adding life to the party until there was no party left.

THE HOT SUN BEAT down on me, turning my bomb suit helmet into an oven. Sweat flowed out of my pores, soaking every square inch of my thick, green suit of armor. The urge to wipe my eyes was unrelenting, but I did my best to ignore it and focus on an eighteen-inch steel pipe with caps at either end.

I noted the size, shape, and dimensions of the small pipe bomb; paying special attention to two small wires that protruded from one end and disappeared into the sandy ground. I struggled under the weight of the bomb suit as I slowly rose up from my kneeling position and began to walk backward. The armor of the bomb suit is strongest across the front, so it was safest for me to face the potentially lethal device for as long as possible.

At a safe distance away from the device, Tyler and the rest of my small team helped me take off the heavy helmet. Tyler offered a water bottle, which I gratefully accepted. I chugged some cool water with hopes of preventing impending fatigue, heat stress, and overall discomfort from clouding my judgment.

At EOD School, where my team and I were taking this important pipe bomb test, a slogan of "initial success or total failure" was beat into our heads. When the consequences of your decisions and actions are potentially life-threatening, there is no room for errors or mistakes.

I relayed everything I could recall about the small bomb to the team. We discussed initial assessments, and then I solicited inputs for a plan of action. This time, I was the team leader, and the decisions were ultimately mine, but every member of my team was every bit as capable as I was, and had taken their turn as the one in the hot seat. In the EOD community, we realize and appreciate the fact that individuals are fallible and make mistakes. We try to curb that tendency by working in teams.

After a few moments of deliberation, we agreed upon an appropriate procedure, and I again donned my helmet. Tyler and the team loaded the tools I would need into a small wagon, much like a child's Radio Flyer. With my mobility constrained by the bulky bomb suit, I awkwardly dragged the wagon back "down range" to a raised bank near the pipe bomb. From the wagon, I retrieved some portable X-ray equipment and much like at the dentist's office, snapped a few X-rays of the pipe bomb.

In 2007, we were still using wet film, so I had to run the negatives back "up range" to my team to have them developed. Tyler rolled the film through a developer before holding up the exposed images so we could take a look. It was easy to see that the wire ran into a blasting cap, which was nestled tightly amongst some sort of explosive inside the length of pipe.

I waddled back down range, and removed a "disruption" tool from my wagon. The tool is essentially a shotgun barrel on an adjustable stand that can be fired remotely. Our plan was to use a shotgun blast of a clay-like substance to apply pressure to one of the end caps, effectively popping the top off, much like you would open a pill bottle with your thumb. In doing this, I was hoping to safely separate all the components of the bomb without an explosion.

I walked around the raised bank, and like a golfer at the Masters, lined up what I hoped to be an optimum shot angle. If the angle was too steep, I might shoot the explosive, which would probably detonate the bomb. If the shot was too shallow, I might miss the bomb altogether.

Finally content with my angle, I walked back behind the raised bank, unspooling my firing wire as I went. Crouching down for cover, I shouted "FIRE IN THE HOLE!" as loud as I could, and initiated the "disruptor." I heard a loud "pop," but not an explosion. A smile crept across my face as I returned to the bomb site and found that the disruptor had worked perfectly!

In my excitement, I momentarily failed to notice the approach of a grim-faced instructor. His age and experience had worn creases into his face, hiding scars that were probably from shrapnel. A thick wad of chew was tucked into his lip, and he spit a glistening glob of saliva into an open water bottle, uttering a unique "pssst" sound. Hearing this sound immediately extinguished my jubilation, and I turned to face my seasoned mentor.

"Lieutenant Snyder," he calmly began in an apathetic Southern drawl. "You executed that drill perfectly, right up until the part where you shot the wrong end of the pipe bomb."

He docked me sixteen points, which meant that I failed the test and would have to return the next day to take it over again.

Just like that, I went from being elated to being deflated. Students were only offered two chances to pass each respective test, and should you fail twice—a "double-tap," as it was called—you would be dropped from the class, or perhaps from EOD School altogether.

I hung my head in disappointment. I knew there was no room for error, and yet I had made a crucial mistake.

THANKFULLY, WE WERE ABLE to pass the retest, which was just one of the nearly once-a-week tests of EOD School. We studied and practiced, then were tested on all manners of explosives: from IEDs and grenades to guided missiles. After earning our clearances, we studied nuclear weapons, and if we passed, moved on to chemical weapons, biological hazards, and eventually underwater explosive ordnance.

By design, the training regimen was extremely intense. Over time, however, I learned how to manage the stress. Eventually, the tests and training became fun, and my EOD School teammates and I learned to thrive under pressure. As our class size shrunk, we grew even closer to one another. By graduation, we were a close-knit, dynamic group of budding warriors.

As we studied and sweat through our training, Tyler became the emotional center of gravity for our class. His incessant optimism and sense of humor kept us all smiling despite the stresses of constant testing.

ALL OF US AT EOD SCHOOL experienced a bad day or two, like my encounter with the pipe bomb. Some of us were evaluated by the staff and put back into training, while in most cases we lost classmates.

Tyler never struggled. He laughed, smiled, and joked just as much on test day as he did at our backyard barbeques, the beach, or while we blew off steam at the many watering holes in nearby Destin, Florida.

On one such occasion, however, when the instructors came in our classroom to announce passes and failures, Tyler's name was listed among the latter. The entire class was shocked, and silently turned to gauge Tyler's reaction to the announcement.

Tyler didn't flinch. He smiled and requested that his performance be re-evaluated. As he discussed his procedures with two different instructors, with all the panache and acumen of a seasoned defense attorney, he pointed out that there was a discrepancy in the reference publications, resulting in the difference of opinion between himself and the instructors.

The instructors had never noticed the error and, upon scrutiny, realized that Tyler was in fact correct, and had not failed the test in the manner they had originally thought. For the remainder of EOD School, Tyler's name was announced among those who had passed each successive evaluation.

FROM A KNEELING POSITION, I slowly reached out with both hands, evaluating my underwater surroundings. My left hand then hit something large and metallic protruding from the floor of the Intracoastal Waterway along the Gulf Coast. This was my team's final examination at EOD School.

I moved my hands across the object's corroded, yet distinctly man-made skin. On either end of the long cylinder, I found tightly nestled loops of thick rope that met in the middle of the large object. I traced out the entire length of the thick rope, ensuring that the "timber hitch" knot was securely and correctly tied.

I traced the rope back to the middle, where it was looped through a heavy metal ring. Attached to the ring was a canvas bag stuffed with an enormous balloon and a set of two SCUBA jugs. The whole ensemble wavered gently, floating in the water column above the large cylinder. I traced out every detail of the gear, at times struggling to feel small details with my gloved fingers. At the junction of the SCUBA tanks and the stuffed canvas bag was a brass fitting about the size of a dinner plate.

At the center of the fitting was a valve that contained a small explosive charge. When a current was run through the valve, the explosive would be triggered, forcefully opening the valve, allowing the three thousand psi of air contained in the SCUBA jugs to fill the enormous balloon. The balloon would then rocket to the surface, lifting the large cylinder, which was an inert training mine. This would allow my team to tow the mine safely ashore, and pass our last test of EOD School.

We couldn't have been training at a more important time. In addition to the ongoing war in Afghanistan, the US military was sending more troops to Iraq in 2007, with the "surge" reaching its peak of one hundred sixty-eight thousand troops just as I was wrapping up my training. That year was also the deadliest of the entire Iraq war for coalition forces, with nine hundred sixty-one troops (nine hundred four of them American) killed in 2007, according to icasualties.org. The same source notes that by the end of 2007, a staggering sixty-three percent of troop deaths were being caused by IEDs. Considering that stark reality, along with the fact that so many innocent civilians were also being killed and maimed by IEDs, EOD School took on an even greater sense of urgency.

Back underwater, I could barely see while trying to inspect my work. The murky depths of the Intracoastal Waterway were filled with massive amounts of silt, which floated all around my mask and gear. Despite the filth, I mentally checked off each step of my procedures as I went about tying knots and piecing together the system that would remove the explosive. Finally content with my setup and ensuing inspection, I found a small reel of firing wire attached to the explosive valve, and began unspooling it as I ascended toward the surface.

As my head broke the surface of the water, I saw Tyler smiling above me as he offered his hand from the side of a rigid hull inflatable boat (RHIB). I grabbed hold, and Tyler yanked me out of the water. As I reported the successful attachment of the "lift balloon apparatus," Tyler inserted the two electric leads of the wire into a small firing device. We had already cleared the area, but Tyler scanned the water around us to ensure there were no other boats present.

"FIRE IN THE HOLE!" Tyler shouted three times.

With my vision finally clearing after exiting the silt-filled waterway, my eyes anxiously darted around the bay waiting to see the giant balloon shoot up. Tyler and I glanced nervously at one another, and finally decided to try the firing device again. Nothing happened, and Tyler shot me a questioning look.

I was sure that I hadn't messed anything up. But either way, I was going back in the water.

I jammed my regulator back in my mouth and flipped over the side of the boat. Just before I reached the bottom of the waterway, the small amount of light I had to work with suddenly disappeared, and I immediately knew it wasn't because of the silt. All of a sudden, a large, looming shadow appeared right in front of me.

The darkness created by the shadow and the silt left me with a sensation I had never felt before. I sensed danger, but couldn't see a thing. It was almost as terrifying as when I imagined the monsters of Weeki Wachee Springs during my first real dive as a little boy. There were no scary sea monsters in Florida's Intracoastal Waterway, either, but not being able to see had me on the verge of panic. Instinctively, I reached for my knife, imagining that the shadow was actually a great white shark, even though I knew it was impossible.

After calming down, I put my knife away and began searching with my hands, as if I were blind. What I found shocked me. The brass fitting at the bottom of the balloon had not been tight enough, and only a small amount of air had made it inside the balloon, which was now out of its bag.

I returned to the surface and reported my findings. After replacing the tanks on my back to make sure I had enough oxygen, I dove back to the depths with a new lift balloon.

While making Darth Vader–like breathing sounds and still battling darkness and silt, I started my meticulous setup and inspection routine all over again. I traced each detail with my fingers before eventually finding the small reel of firing wire. Very carefully, I began unspooling the wire as I once again ascended to the surface.

After another booming set of "fire in the holes," Tyler pressed the fire button with his thumb. Again, I silently scanned the blue water. Nothing happened at first, but before long, I heard Tyler cheer as the giant white balloon burst out of the water on our starboard side. I smiled and let out a sigh of relief as I stripped off my dive gear. My job was done. I enjoyed the short boat ride as my team towed the mine ashore, and thus passed our final exam of EOD School.

We had started the eighteen-month curriculum at Dive School with fifty or so prospective EOD candidates. By the time our class graduated EOD School in September 2007, we had been whittled down to only eight original members, including Tyler, Slider, Pete, Rex, and me. We beamed with pride that morning as we pinned on our EOD "crabs," which signified our joining this elite community as newly minted EOD technicians.

7

A Cut Above

I checked into my first real duty station on December 7, 2007, in beautiful Charleston, South Carolina. It was then that I quickly reached a painful conclusion: despite all of my EOD School training, I had no earthly clue what I was doing.

As I wandered through the compound of EOD Mobile Unit Six, I stuck out like a sore thumb in my dress blues, while everyone else walked around comfortably in green cargo shorts and blue hoodies. Occasionally, someone would recognize the cluelessness on my face and offer some direction. Even while trying to help, though, they would speak in acronyms, which the military is famous for, and leave me even more confused. Not wanting to reveal my confusion, I would just smile, say thank you, and walk away.

After a few more hours, I stumbled upon a door that was marked "CO" for "commanding officer." I knocked, and after receiving permission, I marched into the small office. I was delighted to finally see a familiar face. The tall, curly haired commander in desert fatigues was the same man who sat on the far right of the table during my EOD screening interview at the Naval Academy. After a nice conversation, he graciously invited me to the command's Christmas party, which would also mark the anniversary of the attack on Pearl Harbor.

With my CO's guidance during the ensuing weeks, I started getting a handle on my new job, which I needed to learn quickly. While the "surge" was starting to improve conditions in Iraq, roadside bombs were still the enemy's deadliest tactic on the battlefield, which included the mountains of Afghanistan. As a result, EOD platoons were furiously preparing and heading straight out the door. Many of my new peers had been deployed at least once, with some having served multiple, very dangerous combat tours in both war zones.

I was humbled by the brave men and women around me, while at the same time frustrated that I was still just an ignorant young US Navy ensign. I yearned to be one of the tough guys loading their gear into black bags, throwing on desert fatigues, and heading to the airport to catch the next C-17 bound for Baghdad or Kabul. I was tired of always being in classrooms, listening to stories, looking at pictures, or conducting training scenarios. To be honest, I was ready to start blowing things up.

One morning, I got the news I had been waiting for when a seasoned warrant officer—a living legend in the EOD community—announced that I would be replacing him as the new platoon commander. Needless to say, he left tremendously big shoes to fill, and I didn't feel worthy. But at least I brought both left and right shoes this time.

Only about half the men in that small office would remain with the platoon. Some were reassigned; some opted to end their Navy careers; some ended up serving with the now-famous SEAL Team Six. While our remaining group waited for orders, we meticulously evaluated our gear, identified equipment shortfalls, and developed a training plan for the cycle leading up to our deployment.

One piece of equipment that I liked was a large, fixed-blade knife. It not only looked cool, but I also imagined that it would be handy to have a big knife readily accessible for prepping demolition materials, slicing fruit, or killing bad guys (not necessarily in that order). After fastening a few rifle magazine pouches to my kit, I set about attaching the large knife.

As I pulled the knife out of its sheath, I ran the entire blade across, then through, the tip of my left index finger. I yelped in pain and stupidly shook my hand to ease the pain, causing blood to spray all over the floor, as well as on my new equipment. Then, I felt the tip of my finger wag around loosely as I immediately stopped moving my left hand. Feeling angry and humiliated, I wrapped a paper towel around my finger, sealed it in place with gorilla tape, and began cleaning up my ridiculous mess. I drove myself to the emergency room, and after a few painful hours, my finger was sewn back together.

For the most part, I was able to hide this embarrassing incident, except for from one teammate, Danny, who subsequently noticed my stitches.

"You're a real cut above the rest, aren't you, Snyder?" Danny said in jest.

He laughed heartily as I recalled the whole outrageous story, but to his credit, he kept everything between us.

Danny, who was assigned as my team leader, worked with me on all aspects of our complex job. Each EOD platoon can be broken down into smaller teams, and while on deployment, these teams can individually respond to a myriad of explosive hazard scenarios.

One example is the discovery of a roadside bomb. The EOD community values knowledge over rank in combat situations, and despite my status as an officer, Danny—an enlisted EOD technician—would supervise me. It's rare for such a role reversal to exist inside the Navy, but it's also a point of pride in the EOD community. Experience means more than your uniform's insignia.

As we trained to confront explosive hazard scenarios in Iraq or Afghanistan, Danny would get the team into a security posture, while it was my job to ready the robot that would inspect an enemy IED. I was also the designated robot driver, which at first was a whole new conduit for frustration. The learning curve needed to effectively utilize the robots was very steep. I struggled greatly at first, but Danny's guidance—and patience—remained steadfast.

During our first drill, I ran two robots over a ravine, completely disabling one. After manually recovering the other, I proceeded to get its tracks tangled in a huge mess of rope and firing wire. When we pulled back to the hangar with the robot hanging off the back of the truck, our whole team erupted in laughter.

Despite my failings and friendly ribbing from my teammates, however, I began to improve and earn some level of respect. By the time we were ready to deploy, Danny had shaped me into an adequate team member, for which I was extremely grateful. Still, I was anxious to prove myself on the battlefield.

As America prepared to elect a new commander-in-chief in the fall of 2008, our EOD platoon had assembled. The nine of us then traveled up to Virginia Beach to be evaluated on whether we were suitable for deployment. The week was grueling, and despite a few miscues here and there, our platoon received a favorable grade. Content, we drove back to Charleston amid extreme excitement. Finally, it was our turn to answer the call of duty in Iraq.

WE HAD LITTLE TIME to spare in the following weeks, but I was able to make one last trip home to St. Petersburg to visit my family before I left. My brother, Mitch, was away at school, on his way to earning Hall of Fame honors as one of the best NCAA Division II swimmers in history at Drury University in Springfield, Missouri. My other brother, Russ, was wrapping up his senior year of high school, where it looked like he would most likely graduate as his class's valedictorian. My sister, Elyse, was just beginning middle school, and was emerging as a talented athlete in her own right.

While most of my family maintained a blissful lack of awareness about what I was doing and where I was headed, the reality of my position was not lost on my dad. One night, we stayed up late together while sipping drinks and reminiscing on our backyard patio.

After a while, my dad revealed a sentiment that I will never forget. He told me that he was scared, and he didn't know how to handle being so worried about my safety.

My father told me that he had never imagined such a life for me. He professed that he had been proud of my appointment to the Naval Academy, but he was shocked and dismayed when I picked such a risky job upon commissioning. Instead, he confided that he had always envisioned me as the captain of a ship. In his mind, I would retire after twenty years, and then follow his father into the shipbuilding industry.

My dad didn't know what to make of my role as a bomb technician deploying to Iraq, except that he was extremely frightened about the consequences. With a tear in his eye, he offered one last bit of advice.

"Don't be a hero," he said. "You just come back . . . you hear me?"

I held back my own tears and nodded.

I suppose I didn't really know what to make of me being an EOD technician, either. Of course, I knew my mission, tactics, tools, and procedures, but what about the risks? What if something bad happened? What if a rocket landed on me while I slept? What if my vehicle was struck by an IED? What if a rocket propelled grenade (RPG) hit a helicopter's tail as I rode inside?

As I drifted to sleep that night in Florida, I thought of each member of my family living their lives, going to school, working hard, and trying to be good people. I remembered the Twin Towers smoldering during that awful day in 2001, and reminded myself that there are bad people out there who aimed to harm good Americans like those who made up my family.

With that in mind, I couldn't sit idly by. I could see no other path but to dedicate myself to protecting my family and their way of life. In my mind, any risk that I might take in doing so was well worth it. In the words of US Marine First Lieutenant Travis Manion, a Naval Academy graduate who had been killed in Iraq the previous year, "If not me, then who …"

IN LATE SEPTEMBER 2008, we donned our tan desert fatigues and made last-minute adjustments to our kits, which we then loaded into those black gear bags. My team said goodbye to their families, piled into large, green trucks, and drove to the airfield, where we would soon depart for war. Waiting for us was a large, gray C-17 with its tail ramp open like the jaws of an enormous shark.

We grabbed our bags and wheeled them into a small terminal next to the aircraft. A security guard asked for identification before we could board the flight. I patted my empty front pocket, and my face turned a pale shade of white. I realized that I had forgotten my ID, which prompted my friend Danny to laugh, just like he did when he had found out the story behind my stitches.

I stole the keys to a nearby green truck and tore back to my base like Dale Earnhardt. After finding my ID, I made it back to the departing aircraft with only minutes to spare. I panted heavily, and wiped sweat from my brow as I strapped into a small seat in the cargo bay. The jet's large jaws snapped shut before the aircraft taxied for a moment, accelerated to full speed, and lifted off for the unknown.

All of us settled in and did our best to sleep through the long flight to Germany, and then, to our final destination. I already knew what I would dream about during the flight: being a warrior, which I had been training for since boyhood.

The next time I woke up, however, the dream would be reality. Finally, after six years of Navy training, I was on a flight bound for Baghdad.

8

Inshallah

When I left for Iraq in October 2008, I felt as though I had a very accurate mental image of what warfare would be like. Still, I often wondered how I would handle myself when bullets first started whizzing by. Would I be crippled by fear, or would I be able to rise to the occasion and lead my troops?

I felt my nerves kick in as our aircraft descended sharply toward the airfield in Baghdad. I did my best to hide my trepidation as I strapped on my armor and fastened the chin strap of my helmet. I slid one arm through the sling of my rifle, and loaded a fresh magazine. I rested the webbing of my right hand at the base of my pistol grip, mentally preparing for the impending doom I assumed would certainly greet us upon landing.

A gentle screech of the tires indicated that we were officially on the ground in Iraq. We taxied for a moment, and then all was still. Not saying a word, my teammates and I intently stared at the ramp at the back of the aircraft.

When the aircraft's jaws opened, I saw a giant airstrip laid out before me, illuminated by giant white spotlights that lined each side of the strip. Single man forklifts and front end loaders buzzed all around, shuttling pallets of ammunition, food, and port-o-potties here and there. A thick cloud of dust seemed to hover just above the airfield, which slightly occluded the lights and gave everything between me and the distant horizon an amber glow. I had expected everything to be blacked out entirely, in order to prevent the enemy from being able to pinpoint our location for rocket fire. Instead, it seemed as though I had landed in the middle of a massive space station being built on some strange, tan moon in a distant galaxy.

We waited on the ramp until one of the small forklifts met our aircraft to offload our gear. Then, we were taken into a small room for an introductory lecture. There were three cardinal sins—we were quickly told—for US troops in Iraq:

1. Thou shalt not possess, distribute, or ingest any sort of alcohol.
2. Thou shalt not go anywhere without a loaded weapon.
3. Thou shalt not be caught dead without a standard issue reflective belt.

"Reflective belt?" I quietly wondered aloud.

As though she heard me, the US Army sergeant administering the introductory brief went on to explain that there had been an increased number of fatalities due to pedestrians being struck by armored vehicles on base. The reflective belts marked a concerted effort to curb that trend.

Shortly thereafter, we boarded a small bus, reminiscent of the "party bus" that one of your friends would charter to shuttle a wedding party from the ceremony to the reception. This time, of course, there was no alcohol on board, and instead of laughing during the ride, passengers were worried that the bus might hit a roadside bomb.

An odd mix of American music and brief interludes of Arabic commentary blared from two tiny speakers at the front of the vehicle. The bus then started bouncing up and down on dirt roads. As we hit pothole after pothole, I wondered if they might have been caused by prior explosions.

The shuttle seemed to be on the verge of suffering a mechanical breakdown when it shuddered to a halt in front of a tiny facility built entirely of plywood. We disembarked, and dragged our large black trunks containing our gear and a few changes of clothes to the stoop just outside the small shack.

I stepped inside and checked in with a tired-looking Army sergeant. I was then directed to a collection of large tents adjacent to the small shack. The sounds of our dragging gear disrupted the fitful slumber of the many service members and contractors who occupied the village as we aimlessly wandered around. The village served as a temporary staging area for Americans who were entering or departing Iraq.

We finally found our assigned tent, which was filled with nine cots and a noisy air conditioning unit that barely mitigated the awful desert heat. As I sweat through my first night in Iraq, it finally hit me that I was really going to spend the next six months of my life in this war-torn furnace.

The next morning, we checked in with the EOD command that would serve as our supervision for the deployment. We spent the day meeting staffers and being briefed on the latest operational trends. At the end of our first full day, we were informed that seven of us would hitch a helicopter ride south, while the remaining two would link up with a ground convoy to transport our gear. I would be among those boarding the chopper the next day.

For the second straight night, I struggled to sleep on my hot, uncomfortable cot, mostly due to my excitement for my first helicopter ride in Iraq. My teammates and I would be heading to our assigned Forward Operating Base (FOB) to begin our new mission.

When the first ray of light poked through a small hole in the tent, I leapt off of my cot, put on my boots (appropriate ones for each foot, I'll have you know) and jogged off toward the dining facility. I gorged on an omelet and some fresh fruit, which I relished as I was prepared to eat far worse, and watched my hometown Tampa Bay Rays lose to the Philadelphia Phillies in the fifth game of the 2008 World Series.

While disappointed by how Tampa Bay's magical season had ended, I was too excited to let it get me down. I was finally on deployment.

I jogged back to my tent to find the rest of my guys rolling up their sleeping bags and loading up their gear. Again, we doggedly dragged our big black boxes across the gravel, sweating in our armor and helmets. We loaded up in a different, equally worn down shuttle, which bounced us back to the airfield.

Two slick-looking Black Hawk helicopters were waiting for us, their rotors already spinning. After unloading our gear from the shuttle and onto the two helicopters, we sat in small canvas seats that hung in the snug bay of the aircraft. Two gunners checked our belts and the arrangement of our gear, much like flight attendants making final preparations for a commercial flight. The only difference was that these guys had guns.

They settled in behind their M240 machine guns, donning huge black helmets that resembled those worn by the pilots of TIE fighters in *Star Wars*. Each gunner grabbed hold of the charging handle of their large weapons, jerked backwards, and let go, which slammed a round into the machine gun's chamber. In that exact instant, the aircraft lurched off the ground as if an enormous weight had just been lifted. The helicopters rose in perfect unison, and—as if it were part of an elaborate choreographed dance—turned and accelerated towards the empty desert to the east of Baghdad.

Once clear of the large airfield below, the helicopters banked to the south in an elegant maneuver that sent my stomach (and part of my breakfast omelet) into the back of my throat. As the helicopter banked, I looked to my left, gazing out a window at the ground rushing by. Just as my consideration of the questionable physics governing the flight of a helicopter caused some doubt regarding this precarious position, the chopper jerked upright, and again accelerated. As we tore south, the two helicopters buzzed around each other, mimicking playful dragonflies.

At once, without warning, my aircraft shot skyward, rapidly gaining elevation. My eyes scanned all windows for a clue as to the impetus behind our rapid ascension, but the blue skies gave no such hints. Just as suddenly, we leveled out, and then banked right into a tight circle.

Out of our starboard window, I saw the other helicopter landing on a small soccer field. Dust and scraps were blown upward and outward, which oddly did not deter a crowd of children from running toward the black chopper. I watched from above as one of the gunmen tossed what looked like soccer balls out to the excited Iraqi kids. The happy children ran around with their new soccer balls as the other helicopter once again rose skyward.

Our chopper met its counterpart in a downward spiral, and we continued on to the south. I couldn't help but think about what a stark contrast this was to brutal combat scenes from *Full Metal Jacket* or *Platoon*. While the distribution of soccer balls had not been a part of our military training, I was glad to witness a display of such humanity and charity in a dangerous war zone.

Baghdad's city blocks and streets were soon replaced with green fields and ditches. Before long, the lush fields gave way to more sand than I ever saw while growing up on Florida's beautiful beaches. The only thing interrupting the endless, dried out, and seemingly lifeless desert was an occasional mud hut or palm tree oasis. Soon, even those faded away, and with nothing to look at, I began to doze off.

Just as my head began to make an awkward bob while falling asleep in a strange position, my teammate tapped my arm and pointed into the distance. A small city was protruding from the desolation, and grew in size until we saw an airfield surrounded by large concrete walls. Our Black Hawk helicopters swooped in and planted on the ground just as suddenly as they had lifted off.

WEARING ONLY FLIP FLOPS, black shorts, and a tan T-shirt, I lobbed darts at a board mounted on the front of a small plywood hut that served as our office. The sun was retreating below the horizon, and already, the unbearable heat was giving way to a chilly night. We had been in Al Diwaniyah, Iraq, for about a week, and we were all but settled in.

I sipped coffee from a small Styrofoam cup, as was my post-dinner custom. After a few days at our makeshift base, I had established a routine, and with our gear squared away, we were ready for anything. I would stay up late that night, reading intelligence reports from different parts of Iraq to gain insight into the current tactics and procedures being utilized by insurgents.

Just as one of my darts sunk into the board, a loud blast rocked through the air. I turned to face the direction of its origin, and saw a large cloud of thick smoke about a mile away. Just to the left of the cloud, a second fireball shot into the air, which turned into a second black cloud. I darted inside our office to stand by the phone. One by one, my teammates found their way in as well, and as expected, the phone rang.

Three rockets had detonated close to a police station in the city adjacent to our base. Due to the proximity of the blasts to our walls, it was unclear as to whether the intended target was us or the Iraqi police. In any case, our headquarters requested that my team evaluate the damage, ensure there were no remaining explosives that could pose a threat to civilians, and try to find the attack's point of origin.

Three of my teammates immediately departed while I settled in to man the phones. Basically, I would serve as a middleman between my team in the field and our headquarters. While I wanted to throw on my kit and head out the door, my job as an officer usually meant I would be the guy who manned the phones.

After a few hours, my team returned to report that the damage had been minimal. There had been no significant casualties, and my very capable teammates had been able to locate the point of origin. My men had also retrieved the insurgents' rocket launcher, which was a crude mess of welded metal with a rusted hand crank.

After their surprisingly upbeat report, my team started conducting a forensic analysis of the rail, which would hopefully yield biometric data on who was responsible for the attack. We would then upload the information into a giant database, which was used to target, capture, and prosecute insurgents.

As my team began collecting data, I stared at the rocket launcher my men had found. Just a few short hours ago, two or maybe three Iraqi youths had driven that launcher to a spot in the desert that was just outside the city. They had loaded three rockets and set up a remote timer. They aimed the launcher at the city—or our base—with the intent of indiscriminately killing everyone in its crosshairs. They had probably chattered in excitement as they drove to a spot where they almost certainly hid and watched their terrorist attack unfold.

Now, their instrument of death lay right in front of me. This was the first time that I came face to face with the idea of war. Chills ran down my spine as I considered the fact that those insurgents were still out there, potentially staring at our office with binoculars while they planned their next assault.

UPON OUR OCTOBER 2008 arrival in Iraq, generals, legislators, lawyers, and statesmen were meeting in Baghdad to iron out a new Status of Forces Agreement. Outlined was a plan for US and coalition forces to slowly relinquish command and control over military and municipal matters to a newly established Iraqi government. Unbeknownst to us, the area where we would be sent was also one of the first locations slated to relinquish jurisdiction.

At the time, this was a monumental moment in the war, as well as a sure sign of progress. But it also caused some degree of heartache for my team. We had trained so hard and prepared so well for our mission, but because of the pending agreement, we were effectively benched. Particularly after experiencing that first rocket attack, it was very difficult to stand back, advise, and assist, as we were told to do.

It was a hard pill to swallow, but swallow it we did, and we collectively embraced our new roles as instructors for Iraqi troops. We crafted basic training curriculums, arranged for time at a demolition range to practice safe procedures, and even converted one of our office huts into a classroom to host our Iraqi army counterparts. That part was easy enough, but then in the execution of our task, we faced a whole new set of challenges in the language and cultural barriers between us and the Iraqis.

We only had one interpreter. That worked well in one-on-one situations, but when it came to training exercises or working on the demolition range, we were forced to get very creative. We all did our best to learn little words and phrases, but mostly, we relied on charades. After a while, we got the hang of it, and began building relationships.

I earned a nickname of the Arabic term for "robot." The Iraqis referred to me this way because I was either training Iraqis to dispose of bombs using robots, or trying to convince their leadership to allow me to give robot training.

In working with Iraqi leaders, I learned another Arabic word very quickly: inshallah, which essentially means "God-willing." The word was not only spoken all the time by Iraqis, but truly embodied our cultural differences. To them, punctuality was not important, as they would arrive whenever God willed them to arrive. This was, on average, fifteen to thirty minutes after the agreed upon time. It was also difficult to convince the Iraqis to do any actual training, because God had seemingly provided them with a long list of excuses, whether it was having tea or sleeping in. To us, "inshallah" seemed to be a convenient way to put off a day's work until tomorrow.

The worst of this stigma came about when we reviewed the Iraqi army's EOD tactics. After running a few fictional drills on their leadership, we were shocked to find that their default solution to most potential explosive hazards was to equip one of their most junior soldiers with a small set of pliers before sending him downrange to manually dismantle the device. Should the device detonate during this process, well … that was God's will. Inshallah.

At first, it was very difficult to convey to the Iraqis that by using robots, long lengths of rope or creative tactics, a soldier can protect himself, while still safely mitigating the potential hazard. After banging our collective heads on the wall for a while, the Iraqis finally began to see the benefit of the philosophical issues in our teachings.

SOMEWHERE IN BETWEEN SLEEP and wake, I lay on my bed and listened. My eyes still closed, I could hear the drip, buzz, and gurgle of my programmed coffee pot on the desk next to my bed. I reached out further and could hear a small rodent or bird scratching up some breakfast beneath my small trailer. I could hear the mechanical whine of my AC unit, singing in unison with the units installed above the windows of my teammates' trailers. I heard the slam of someone's door as they exited their trailer. I heard my teammate shuffle to the toilet at the end of our row, his boots dragging across the loose gravel.

For a moment, all was still. I thought about how strange it was to be so comfortable this far from home. I had built this experience up in my mind, expecting constant battle, austere conditions, and intense stress. Instead, I had my own trailer, outfitted with a coffee pot, a laptop computer with Internet, and no real combat to speak of. I smiled and began stretching in preparation for getting out of bed.

The stillness was interrupted by another sound, similar to a door slamming, but slightly different. It was distant, but vaguely familiar. Creases formed on my forehead as I tried to remember where I had heard that sound before. The sound repeated: just louder, just closer. At the exact moment I recognized the sounds as explosions, a rocket ripped through the air a few feet above my trailer.

It screamed as it flew; its flight punctuated with a loud boom as it detonated less than one hundred meters away. I leapt from my bed, threw on a hoodie, darted out the door, and dove towards the sandbag bunker in front of my trailer. One of my teammates had the same idea, and we comically slammed into each other on the way.

As we took cover, we heard one more explosion before an eerie silence. One by one, my teammates shouted from their respective bunkers, and once I had accounted for my men, I took off towards the office to field the impending phone call. Again, my team was tasked with evaluating the damage, while also attempting to locate the point of origin. There were four reported detonations: three on our base, and one just outside the wall. I divvied up the tasks and dispatched my team into the combat zone.

One rocket had struck a small airfield on the north side of our base and caused no damage. Nearby, another rocket had nearly missed the base, also causing no damage. A third rocket had landed in the middle of a parking lot, and even though there were thirty to forty American soldiers sleeping within fifty meters, no one was hurt. Aside from a few flat tires, punctuated by blast fragments, damage was surprisingly minimal.

The last impact, though, was the rocket that had flown directly over our row of trailers. The rocket had barely cleared a large wall of portable HESCO barriers—made of heavy duty fabric fortified by metal wiring—before going behind our office and hitting a trailer on the other side. The trailer had served as an office for one of the many civilian contractors that worked on our base. The rocket had struck the bottom of the trailer, near the corner where its long axis met its short one.

As the rocket landed, a small fuse on its nose was crushed, initiating a small chain of rapid explosions that escalated within the warhead. This culminated in the detonation of the main charge, when approximately ten pounds of military grade explosives erupted into a large fireball that consumed everything within about three feet. As the fireball leapt up and out, it sent fragments of the warhead's now shattered steel casing in all directions. The bits of steel absorbed massive amounts of heat and energy from the explosion, and glowed like red-hot embers as they flew through the air, ripping apart anything that got in the way.

As the embers slowed, they bounced off the harder objects in the room, causing slight variations in their path of destruction. In a fraction of a second, the fireball collapsed into a cloud of gray, acid-smelling smoke that lingered like the wraith of death evaluating his handiwork.

The searing steel fragments found their final resting spots, setting fire to stacks of paper, upholstery, and carpet fibers. They melted plastic and etched black scorch marks into anything made of wood. When the smoke cleared, the rocket had left behind a near perfect star of damage, which radiated outward from the point of impact. The core of the star was a near-spherical void cut by the initial blast, from which scorch marks and holes clearly outlined the paths of many blast fragments.

There was a desk at the far end of the room that had been shredded by lethal projectiles of glowing steel. Smoldering paper muttered to itself as it slowly burned. A chair rested slightly askew behind the tattered desk, riddled with smoking holes.

Every other morning for the previous six months, a contractor had woken up to the sound of his alarm clock at 0430. He would yawn as he pulled on his jeans, and then his boots. He would then pour himself a cup of coffee before stepping outside to make the short walk to his office. He would step inside and pull the door closed, then ease himself into his office chair. The contractor would then flip open his laptop computer and would usually begin composing an e-mail to his family back home. He would then begin to slog his way through his many work e-mails, sketching out the day's to-do list.

At 0510 that particular morning, he just happened to glance down at an empty coffee cup. He decided to head to the cafeteria to grab a new cup before returning to resume his workday.

As he dumped a packet of sugar into his coffee, the rocket struck his trailer, destroying his office and sending blast fragments tearing through the spot where he had sat not even five minutes earlier.

No one was killed that day. No one was even hurt. I personally believe that the word "miracle" is overused, but as I stared wide-eyed at what was left of that trailer, I was convinced that the contractor's survival was indeed some sort of miracle.

My team and I spent the day conducting analyses of the attack. We compiled reports, took pictures, and gathered fingerprints and blast fragments. I briefed the leadership of the base, and answered as many questions as I could.

As the sun dipped below the barren horizon, I returned to my room for the first time that day. I melted into my desk chair, exhausted from the day's events. As I stared at some Christmas lights and sipped coffee, the sparing of the contractor occupied my thoughts. I couldn't get past how close that man had been to death. I thought about how that same rocket had passed over each of my teammates' trailers. Death had come looking for us, but had just missed. Was it a coincidence? Was it a warning? Again, I don't normally subscribe to any sort of destiny or fate, as I believe that we largely make our own way through the world. I just couldn't get past the immensity of this particular coincidence, though.

As I mulled it over, this inexplicable feeling of freedom washed over me. It was as if I had been liberated of some unknown burden, some expectation of something that I hadn't realized was there. For a moment—just a moment—there was only me, the coffee, my chair, and the lights. There was no yesterday. There was no tomorrow. Just there; right then and there.

In that moment, I was at peace with myself, and at peace with the world. Somehow, contemplating the end of things, and coming face to face with grave danger had allowed me to understand that nothing else mattered. By considering and acknowledging death's existence and my lack of control over it, I finally understood and accepted my mortality. It was a very strange feeling of helplessness and insignificance, yet also comforting and warm.

It was as though instead of fighting against the rules of the world, I had learned to live in harmony with them. As I set down my coffee and rocked myself to sleep in my chair, I was at peace with whatever would happen during the rest of my first combat deployment.

Inshallah.

9

The Toll of War

A few months later, Tara, who I dated for seven months at the Naval Academy and subsequently stayed in touch with, was waiting to see me at her parents' home on the beautiful Chesapeake Bay. Her gorgeous eyes, which had captivated me ever since I first saw them in Annapolis, sparkled in the firelight as she smiled and welcomed me home from Iraq.

As we curled up together in a giant hammock, Tara and I caught up on the previous six months. Under an immaculate starry sky, we eventually fell asleep to the gentle sounds of a dying fire and the tide lapping at the shore.

In the morning, we left that comfortable house and both headed back to busy and, unfortunately, separate lives. She returned to Quantico, Virginia, where she was attending The Basic School, which all US Marine officers must complete. I was headed to Virginia Beach, where I had been reassigned after my deployment to Iraq.

This sort of thing had been going on for the past four years. Tara and I had "officially" dated for the better part of my senior year, but she broke up with me as I departed Annapolis for Dive School. She had two years left as a midshipman, and believed that a long-distance relationship would be too difficult for either of us to maintain.

She may have been right, but I was very much in love, and vowed to persist. I knew that her feelings for me also lingered, and despite opposing career paths, we continued to find excuses to meet up. We made little weekend trips to New York to visit her family or catch a show. We visited monuments and museums in Washington, D.C., or went antique shopping in Fredericksburg, Virginia.

In each other's company, everything seemed magical, but then, we would always have to return to our jobs, which is typical in so many military relationships. Both of us were too driven—or too stubborn, perhaps—to sacrifice our careers to be together. In any case, I was sure that Tara was the most amazing woman that I would ever meet. I hoped that our paths would meet again someday, and perhaps coincide forever.

WHEN I CHECKED INTO my new command, I wasn't nearly as clueless as I had been only a year and a half ago. I had a few more pieces of flair (not the *Office Space* kind!) above my left breast pocket, and along with those uniform ribbons came a little confidence. After going through pre-deployment training and six months of being an EOD officer in Iraq, I was at least comfortable enough to find my own way around a new compound. It didn't take long to settle in, especially after finding some familiar faces.

After a few mostly idle weeks, I was pleased to learn that I had been assigned to a new EOD platoon, which was in Iraq. After they returned, I would replace the officer in charge (OIC) and embed with SEAL Team Ten on subsequent missions. Working with Navy SEALs as an explosives specialist was a dream come true, and while

I knew it would be dangerous, I couldn't wait to deploy with them to Afghanistan or Iraq.

I was even more pleased to learn that Tyler, who I had bonded so closely with at EOD School, was already assigned to this platoon. So not only would I be doing my dream job, I would be working alongside one of my best friends. I was so excited.

The only negative aspect of the assignment, if there was one, was waiting six months for SEAL Team Ten to return before we could begin training for the next deployment, which would likely start in the spring of 2011. I didn't like the idea of so much downtime before another combat tour, but at least I knew it would be worth the wait.

I left work early that day to settle into my new Virginia Beach condo. Over the next few days, I caught up with my old teammates, who were also getting acclimated to new assignments and settling into new homes. While at a backyard barbecue with my buddy Sam, I was presented with a welcome-home gift from his young son, Ethan. Like his dad, Ethan was strong, bright, and possessed a seemingly endless supply of energy. After learning that I was living alone, the five-year-old opened a small, blue lunchbox. Inside was a turtle that he had caught nearby, which he said would be my new pet.

Honored by young Ethan's sentiment, I set out the next morning to find a terrarium that would be appropriate for my new companion. More difficult than finding the terrarium was deciding which Teenage Mutant Ninja Turtle to name him after. While driving home from the pet store, my mind was going back and forth between the names Raphael, Michelangelo, Donatello, and Leonardo.

As I settled on Donatello, my cell phone began to buzz and chime in my pocket. The screen displayed the name Caleigh, who was my friend Tyler's longtime girlfriend. Perhaps she knew that her boyfriend and I had been assigned to the same platoon, and was calling to talk about it? Or maybe she just wanted to welcome me home and catch up while Tyler was busy in Iraq.

When I first heard Caleigh's voice, though, it was quivering.

"What's wrong?" I said.

There was a brief moment of silence.

"Tyler was killed in Iraq yesterday," Caleigh quietly replied. "We just found out this morning."

After a few moments of confusion, I figured there had to be some sort of mistake. Now that I was assigned to the same platoon, surely I would've already heard if there had been a casualty. Right?

"Are you sure? How can you be sure?" I said as my panic began to increase. Could this really be true?

"The Navy came to notify his mother," Caleigh said, sounding like she was on the verge of tears, if not crying already. "I'm sure."

Bewildered, I gave Caleigh my deepest condolences and thanked her for having the courage to call while she was still processing her own grief. After we got off the phone, I sank into my rocking chair as my world began to spin. I felt numb, dizzy, disconnected, and nauseous.

Time seemed to stop, as if the sounds of the outside world were fading into distant and irrelevant static. I stared at the wall in front of me while rocking my little blue recliner. The walls of my new condo seemed to stare back at me, as though I were a stranger. I started to feel like an impostor in a reality that wasn't mine. Tyler's death was such an unforeseen, unbelievable, abhorrent reality that it caused me to doubt everything that I had trusted to be true. Everything I had built my life around now seemed to quiver and shake as my life's foundations began to crumble.

United States Navy Explosive Ordnance Disposalman Second Class Tyler J. Trahan made the ultimate sacrifice on April 30, 2009,

in Iraq's Al Anbar Province, which was one of the most violent the-
aters of the Iraq war. He was killed by an enemy roadside bomb and
posthumously awarded both the Bronze Star with a "V" for valor and
the Purple Heart. Tyler was only twenty-two years old when he died.

As my mind's eye wandered across memories of Tyler, I experienced grief's full gamut for the first time. Sometimes I would linger
on a feeling of remorse, then transition immediately into raucous
laughter as I relived a funny moment that I had experienced with
Tyler. Sometimes, I would feel multiple emotions all at once, which
led me to sob while attempting to sift through the chaos filling my
head and heart. I rode the waves as they hit me, and after a while,
the tide's power seemed to wane.

After about three days, I found that I was able to manage the
emotions I felt and at least avoid the very worst pain. I did so by
becoming numb, stoic, and almost laconic as I attempted to rejoin
the outside world.

Before I knew it, I was sitting across from Tyler's grieving mother
at a small circular patio table in Bedford, Massachusetts. As we
sat on the deck, the devastated Gold Star mother asked—usually
through tears—that we keep telling stories about her departed son.
Somehow, through the vivid recollections of his friends and fellow
Navy sailors, Tyler seemed to come back to life, if only for a fleeting
moment.

I sat in the back of the funeral home while Tyler's family and
friends paid their respects at his closed, flag-draped casket. Hundreds, if not thousands, waited in long lines to share just a few words
with Tyler's family, and also to be in the presence of this fine young
American warrior for one last time.

Under the watchful eye of the Patriot Guard Riders, a group of
leather-clad motorcyclists who travel from afar to protect the sacred
burials of American troops killed in action, the line ambled through

the small funeral home. For nearly eight hours, Tyler's family courageously stood and gratefully accepted condolences, stories, and well-wishes from all who had been touched by their fallen hero's life.

After the wake, I stood outside at a party being held in Tyler's honor, as we were all sure that such a gathering was precisely what he would have wanted. As I sipped flavorless beer from a red plastic cup, I listened to Tyler's newest teammates, as well as classmates from EOD School, share emotional stories about how they learned of his death. I watched and listened as big, strong, brave men completely lost control of their emotions.

Later that night, I stood against the wall in a cold, concrete garage. Some of Tyler's grieving friends had started playing beer pong, which reminded me of the fun, memorable night during EOD School when Tyler made a beer pong table for us out of scrap wood.

As the group of friends played beer pong games in Tyler's honor, many spoke noisily, drunkenly, and emotionally as they shared memories of the young man that all of us missed so much. As I looked around the room at so many people who had known and loved Tyler, I felt even closer to my friend. Everywhere I looked, I could see his face. As others laughed, I could hear Tyler laugh, too.

Despite the comfort of being among Tyler's best friends, it became even harder to accept that he was gone. How could someone so full of life—so positive, so dedicated, so virtuous, so good—be taken away? I suppose I already knew the answer, especially after realizing how little control I had over my own fate during those rocket attacks in Iraq. But that still didn't answer the most important question: why did this happen?

I don't have a single ensuing memory from the weeks that followed Tyler's funeral. At one point or another, I know that I returned to work and found a way to occupy my mind. I ran away from my many questions about this great injustice, while trying to counter my grief by immersing myself in work. I spent countless hours at my new EOD compound studying tools, tactics, and procedures. I spent long hours in the gym, in the pool, or outside while running. I did all that I could to escape being alone with my thoughts.

Every once in a while, especially on long runs, I would let my mind wander back to memories of Tyler. I would think about his smile and laugh, but most importantly, his way of being. He was always positive. He always saw the best in things and people. He truly connected with everyone that he met, and everyone that he met loved him.

"Petty Officer Tyler Trahan was an exemplary leader and exceptional EOD technician," Commander Joseph Polanin of Explosive Ordnance Disposal Mobile Unit Twelve said in a statement shortly after Tyler was killed. "Our hearts go out to his family and friends in this very difficult time.

"He was a great warrior, teammate, and friend to so many," my new commanding officer continued. "His patriotic spirit will live on in each of us. His supreme sacrifice will not be in vain."

Indeed, I knew that while I would miss Tyler for the rest of my life, I would do everything in my power to live, learn, and serve my country in a way that would keep his memory alive.

10

Shattered Dream

On the ground in front of me, I stretched out the straps of a large black pack that contained two parachutes: a main and a reserve. I looked over each strap and buckle to ensure that everything appeared to be in good working order. I checked the risers of the main canopy, as well as the cutaway mechanism that might need to be utilized if the main parachute got tangled up during its deployment.

Content that the chute looked to be in good shape, I slipped the leg straps over my thighs and pulled them tight. I repeated the process with the shoulder straps, then stood and stretched into an arched position to check the tightness of the straps. I strapped an altitude meter to my left hand, and then clipped on a lightweight skateboarding helmet with goggles attached. After getting a "thumbs up" and a pat on the behind from my instructors, I sat down on a long bench with a row of others, who were dressed just as I was.

After a moment or two, a small, twin-prop plane landed on a narrow airstrip and taxied to our end of the runway. Instructors wearing parachutes nearly half the size of ours came to meet us, and escorted us to the side door of the aircraft. As the smallest guy in the group, I climbed aboard first, followed by about a half dozen classmates in ascending size order. Our San Diego-based parachute jumping class was comprised of US Special Operators from all branches of service. There were Navy EOD technicians, Navy SEALs, Air Force parachute jumpers, and even an Air Force weatherman.

Once the students and instructors had jammed inside the aircraft, its propellers came to life. The instructors signaled for us to put on our seat belts, which struck me as odd since our intent was to jump out of the plane.

The aircraft's nose tilted upward as we leapt off the ground to fourteen thousand five hundred feet. An instructor then slid the door open, and after a safety check, signaled that the first group of jumpers could stand and approach the door. As the shaking plane began to empty, my stomach was in my throat, much like my first helicopter ride in Iraq.

When it was my turn to jump, my instructor and I were the only ones left on the plane, except for the pilot, of course. I stood, approached the door, and grabbed hold of a bar that ran vertically along the side of the door. I put my toes to the edge and looked down at what appeared to be an intricately drawn map below me. The ocean and the earth looked surreal, as it was littered with mountains that looked like anthills, as well as buildings that looked like LEGOs instead of Southern California landmarks. Fear and trepidation mounted as I considered what I was about to do. I closed my eyes.

My father's words of encouragement echoed through my head as I leapt out of the plane. I extended my arms and arched my back as the air caught my body. As my downward velocity increased, the gravity gave me the sensation of sliding down a hill. After a few seconds, my body settled into a free fall toward the rapidly approaching ground. Strangely, though, it actually didn't feel like I was going anywhere. It truly felt as though I was flying.

I had a huge smile on my face when my instructor thankfully gave me a reminder signal to look at my altimeter. At five thousand five hundred feet, I waved my hands behind my head, grasped the pull cord on my chest, and pulled. For a second, nothing seemed to happen, but just as more fear crept into the back of my head, the parachute's outstretched canopy jerked me upward before I landed safely. I had done it.

AFTER A MONTH OF taking off on planes that I didn't land with, I boarded a jet that took me from San Diego back to the East Coast. I dumped my gear in my Virginia Beach condo's living room, and promptly set out to see if I could catch a few waves. It was nice to take a break and relax at the beach before having to repack for yet another training trip. I would be heading to a place I used to live, Reno, for mobility training, which was essentially comprised of driving Humvees up and down mountains. After Nevada, I would head to Mississippi to learn more about advanced combat shooting techniques and how to handle close-quarter combat situations with enemy insurgents.

During these exciting training stints, I noticed a major difference between myself and most of the SEALs. The frogmen (as SEALs are often called) I worked with were much larger in stature than I was. They could lift heavy loads and carry them for incredibly long distances. My collegiate swimming career, while very enjoyable, had definitely not prepared me to wear heavy helmets, chest and back plates, and a "ruck" (or backpack) with twenty to forty pounds of gear, all while also carrying a rifle and pistol. While I would become quickly exhausted by lugging around so much stuff, the powerful frogmen often made me feel like I was the weakest link.

While immensely respectful of the SEALs, I still didn't enjoy being outperformed. I asked around and did some research, and found that a lot of SEALs were doing Crossfit-style workout programs. Driven by my competitive nature, I began a weight training regimen at a local gym. Before long, I had gained about fifteen pounds of mostly muscle, and noticed that the burden of my gear wasn't as challenging as before.

I HAD JUST RETURNED home from a tough workout when I received a phone call from a Navy swimming teammate, Ed, who was also a mutual friend of my ex-girlfriend, Tara. It was a little out of the ordinary for him to be calling, but I welcomed the chance to catch up, and answered the phone with excitement.

Without giving Ed a chance to talk, I began enthusiastically filling him in on my last few months of combat training. He didn't say much in response, which led me to suspect that something was wrong. My stomach turned as my mind flashed back to that terrible phone call I received to inform me that Tyler had been killed in Iraq. Was another friend of mine killed in action, perhaps from the Naval Academy this time?

"Brad, I know this will be upsetting," Ed solemnly said. "But I wanted you to hear this from me.

"Tara took her own life last night," he continued, to my utter disbelief. "We don't know much except that she was found this morning."

I don't recall what I said to Ed before hanging up. My world was already spinning. After pouring a large glass of wine, I stumbled through my condo before collapsing in the same rocking chair I was sitting in when I learned of Tyler's death. Once again, the foundations around me seemed to crumble, and my grip on the outside world temporarily slipped away.

I drowned myself in that wine glass and didn't come up for about a week.

I didn't understand what had happened or why. As my chair rocked, I thought of Tara and me swaying to sleep on that Chesapeake Bay hammock, shortly after I returned from Iraq. While we resumed leading separate lives after that special evening by the fire, my feelings for Tara never changed. I just couldn't comprehend that she was gone.

I didn't attend Tara's funeral. I couldn't. It hurt too much.

It devastated me to know that whatever was going through Tara's head that final night was so painful that she decided to leave her family and friends. Even after Tyler's death, I still couldn't imagine that level of despair.

Tara had kept a few mementos that I had given her over the years. Eventually, I mustered the courage to go face her parents and collect them. As I eased my truck up the long driveway to the same house on the Chesapeake Bay, I was nearly overcome with emotion. Not wanting to add to the pain of Tara's mother, I clenched my jaw and vowed to be strong as she greeted me at the door. She was sobbing.

I spent the next few hours telling stories, going through Tara's things, and commiserating in grief with her parents. Those hours were among the most emotional and difficult of my life. As the sun went down, I loaded up my truck and drove back to Virginia Beach in silence.

Tara and I weren't a couple when she died, but I had still dreamed of once again being her boyfriend—or perhaps even more—someday. That dream was now over, and Tara's tragic death would stay with me forever.

11

Under the Influence

Tara's death, like Tyler's, seemed to cast a large shadow over my life. Like a looming storm cloud, thoughts of her seemed to occlude all light, which was only exacerbated by the oncoming winter of 2010.

Focusing on my job helped to block out thoughts of losing Tara and Tyler. For the most part, I was successful in keeping the ghosts away, but when things calmed down or got quiet, I would feel Tara's ethereal presence, in particular. I wouldn't say she haunted me, but it was definitely painful. After some time, the pain dulled, and while the clouds didn't recede, I got used to their presence. I began working very long hours so that I wouldn't have to go home to face my thoughts. At the same time, I knew how important it was to make sure my team was ready to deploy.

BY THIS POINT IN MY CAREER, I was eligible to be evaluated as an EOD warfare officer, which was a higher qualification than my status at the time. It would entitle me to wear a different badge, and more importantly, validate my standing within the Special

Operations community as a Subject Matter Expert (SME) in the field of explosive mitigation. First, however, I would have to pass a difficult EOD board, which was similar in nature to my initial examination at the Naval Academy.

In preparation, I spent nearly a month holed up in my office studying different publications and manuals. I was confident when the day of my board finally came, but as soon as the questioning began, I was grilled by my CO and others.

As I got the first set of questions wrong in a rather embarrassing fashion, beads of sweat began to trickle downward in torrents. Before I could dwell on my failures, though, I was on to the next set of questions. My heart rate elevated, and it quickly felt like I was breathing into a bag. Still, I continued to field their questions, frequently darting over to a whiteboard on the boardroom's side wall to sketch diagrams, make calculations, or to illustrate my understanding of a specific concept.

After more than two grueling hours, it all came down to a presentation related to classified and sensitive material. By then, my uniform was drenched in sweat. Thankfully, though, my experiences in Iraq helped me feel comfortable while dealing with the topic at hand. By the end of my remarks and two follow-up presentations, I felt self-assured. After being ushered to an outside room, I took a very deep breath while the board made its decision.

With a loud creak, the conference door popped open, and one of the board members summoned me back inside. I stole glances at their faces, which gave away nothing. The board members appeared pensive, yet stoic, and I was left with no idea as to what they had been speaking about. Had they discussed passing me? Had they focused on my shortcomings, and since become convinced that I wasn't qualified?

I returned to my position at the front of the room, which was behind a podium to the right of the large presentation screen. I stood tall, locked my jaw, and silently affirmed to embrace the out-come like a man: pass or fail.

By the time my CO finished summarizing my presentations and the board's reaction to them, I was sure he was about to sentence me to another year as a basic EOD technician. As I considered my apparent failure, I wanted to look at the floor instead of what was essentially my judge and jury. I managed to fight this urge, however, and resolved to take my lickings. No matter what my CO said next, I would show no defeat.

"Considering all we have outlined, the board and I have decided that our decision is very clear," my CO said in a quiet, almost mono-tone voice. "We have no choice but to pass you."

Because he spoke so flatly, I almost misinterpreted his statement. Once I realized what he had just said, a huge smile crept across my face. I had passed.

Finally, the board members also dropped their masks and smiled. One by one, they offered their congratulations. I was exhausted, but also ready to celebrate. Soon, I would be officially pinned and rec-ognized as one of America's newest EOD warfare officers.

TO MARK THE OCCASION, my team met me at a bar near my condo for dinner. Most of my teammates brought their wives, which made the evening feel like a family affair.

I was on top of the world, and felt so proud of what I had just accomplished. I felt like I had proven myself to a community of war-riors that I respected and valued so much. I looked around at my teammates and saw friends that I had been working, sweating, and bonding with for the past year and a half. It was an honor to sit among men who were well-trained and ready to head off to war, as well as their wives, who were also making tremendous sacrifices.

Deployment was now just weeks away, and while my team was heading to Afghanistan, some of my friends were heading elsewhere. Barring a terrible tragedy, I knew I would see all of these guys again, but still, it felt like we were enjoying one of our last nights on the town before going our separate ways.

If there was ever a time to let loose, this was it. While dealing with the grief of losing Tara and Tyler, I had somehow managed to hold it together long enough to pass my boards and get my marching orders to help lead brave US troops into battle. After raising my beer mug in celebration, I pounded what remained of my beverage before ordering another round.

After dinner, a few more beers, and a trip to the restroom, I returned to the table to find my dinner plate replaced with a beautiful scotch decanter and two matching glasses. My friends also gave me a ball cap emblazoned with the troop patch of the SEAL platoon I was working with. The patch paid homage to brotherhood forged by combat. The decanter and scotch glasses had our EOD badge etched in the glass, along with our platoon number.

That moment was so powerful that I had to fight back tears, but I couldn't cry in front of my teammates. I was so moved by their sentiments, though, because in a way, they were acknowledging my success as their success. They were proud of me as their teammate and as their brother. In that moment, I realized that the significance of my new qualification was meaningless without the respect of my brothers in arms. I will always remember that moment.

High on life and consumed by emotion, I charged even further into the night. Dinner wrapped up, and some of my teammates and their wives went home, while a few of us went to another bar to make fools of ourselves singing karaoke. Eventually, the bar's lights came on as it began to close down. My teammates and I said farewell as they all jammed into a cab.

While waving goodbye, I must have reasoned—through an alcohol-induced haze—that because I needed my car the next morning, I would make the drive home. It was less than a mile, and surely, I could concentrate long enough to successfully navigate my truck to its parking space at my condo. After so much good fortune earlier in the day, what could possibly go wrong on such a glorious evening?

The rest of my memories from that night would later come back to me like random images that emerge from darkness. I remember street and car lights looking strange against the road's freshly fallen snow. I remember blinking rapidly as I struggled to see the yellow lines. I remember swerving into another vehicle, the crunch of metal and shattered glass from the glancing blow, then losing control of my truck and crashing into the shoulder. I remember getting out of my truck to evaluate the damage. I remember being thankful to see the driver and passenger exit their vehicle safe and unharmed, but then being deeply embarrassed as they shot me confused, angry looks. I remember being shocked as I recognized that my truck was most likely totaled. I remember the flashing red and blue lights of the police cruiser that showed up shortly afterward.

I remember the cold steel of the handcuffs that were locked in place on my wrists. The arresting officer told me I was being charged with driving under the influence (DUI).

First and foremost, I was thankful that nobody in the other vehicle was hurt. When my thoughts eventually turned to the gravity of my own situation, however, I hung my head in despair. In less than fifteen minutes, I had all but thrown away a life and career that I had spent nearly a decade building.

I had been given every opportunity to make the right choice, but I was blinded by my own stupidity. Whether due to arrogance or ignorance, I must have believed that I was not required to follow the same rules as everyone else. Somehow, I thought I was smarter, more capable, or maybe just luckier. Whatever was the source of my hubris, it became almost immediately clear that I needed to learn a very difficult lesson.

As I lay on a cot in an extremely cold jail cell, I hated myself for endangering all the innocent people who were on the road that night. I shuddered as I considered what I could have done to the other vehicle's passengers with my reckless and impaired driving. I hated myself for having taken such a foolish risk.

That night, my self-loathing ate away at my self-image until there was nothing left. I was trapped inside a body I no longer loved, in a life that I no longer cared for. My despondency was so complete that there was no room left for any emotion. I wanted to cry, but I didn't think I deserved to pity myself. Still, I wallowed in this despair until my teeth chattered from lack of warmth, both in my jail cell and body.

When I was released from jail in the morning, I rushed straight into work to inform my chain of command that I had been arrested. I knew that their reaction—and the ensuing process—would be painful, as it should have been. Still, I wanted to deploy to Afghanistan with my team. If there was even a single delicate thread of hope left, I wanted to do everything possible to avoid letting my men down more than I already had.

I clung to that thread of hope with all the vigor of a desperate man. I became convinced that the only way to redeem myself—and repair my damaged reputation—would be in combat. I never thought that I would look to the mountains of Afghanistan for salvation, but after my stupid and dangerous mistake, that's exactly where my eyes had turned.

I spent the following few weeks feverishly dealing with both my civil DUI charge and my corresponding punishment under the Uniform Code of Military Justice (UCMJ).

After many months of training in conjunction with SEAL Team Ten, I knew that I was uniquely qualified to help fulfill our mission in Afghanistan. I had all the necessary qualifications, had thoroughly studied the mission, and knew all the people I would be working with on deployment. We were also severely under-manned, meaning that there wasn't really anyone who could take my place if I was suddenly removed as the officer in charge of Pla-toon Twelve-Seven.

Still, my Navy chain of command usually took a very hard stance against offenders like me. Even though it felt like a knife in my chest to even think about, I wondered if my military career was over. While it was a sickening feeling, I knew that there would be no one to blame for that possible outcome but myself.

Then, the awful situation that I created got even worse when I realized that Pete, my EOD school roommate who had just returned from another deployment, would probably be sent in my place. At that point, my resolve to convince my command to let me deploy became stronger than ever. While I could live with being kicked out of the military, I couldn't live with seeing my friend get injured or killed because of my foolish decision.

I told anyone and everyone who would listen that I didn't care what happened to me or my career. All I wanted was the oppor-tunity—or privilege, really—to deploy with my team. I owned my failure and was deeply ashamed of it. But as I told my commanders, I had learned a valuable lesson that I would carry with me to Af-ghanistan and beyond.

Despite the fact that the full ramifications of my DUI and the ensuing letter of reprimand were yet to be resolved, my CO realized that the administrative review would take quite some time. Six weeks later, I learned that my CO and his executive officer (XO) had stuck out their necks and pleaded on my behalf to their superiors.

Given the high demand for EOD techs in Afghanistan and a short supply of qualified officers, my CO decided to allow me to deploy, even though my overall fate as a naval officer would remain firmly in doubt. I was immensely thankful for his vote of confidence in me, and I resolved not to let him or my platoon down. When the next flight to Afghanistan left Virginia Beach, I would be on it. Even though I didn't deserve such good fortune, it was the best news of my life.

12

Fields of Fire

In the dead of night, a CH-47 Chinook helicopter banked sharply from side to side as it maneuvered through a narrow mountain valley in volatile southern Afghanistan, keeping a safe distance from the large rock outcroppings on either side. The Chinook followed an erratic, unpredictable flight path in an effort to avoid potential Taliban RPGs.

From inside the dark helicopter, I gazed out over the lip of the rear loading ramp. Through my NODs, I observed a strange, Martian-green landscape rush by at a blinding speed.

From an earbud jammed into my left ear, I heard the voice of my team leader for this mission, a SEAL named George, say "two minutes." We were approaching our designated landing zone.

Rising to one knee, I unclipped the small karabiner that was the only thing holding me in the rocking helicopter. While creeping closer to the ramp and squinting my eyes, I began studying the terrain buzzing by in an attempt to orient myself. The helicopter then came to a hover and descended over a large farm field just to the south of our target village.

As if it were on cue, the rotor wash kicked up a giant dust cloud, completely obscuring everything from my view except for the ramp in front of me. I felt the aircraft slam into the ground, and the ramp began to lower.

I leapt out, struggling to maintain my balance as my footing shifted from the moving helicopter to the soft, fertile soil of the farm field. The field was made up of about two dozen rows of mounded dirt covered with dense grape vines. Two steps from the ramp, my body sunk down into one of the troughs between two rows of mounded dirt. I hadn't seen the dip due to the thick grape vines and the dust that I was still clearing from my eyes.

I almost fell over as I struggled to maintain my balance in the soft soil, but somehow, I surged forward and avoided being trampled by the remainder of the assault team pouring out of the Chinook behind me. I ran forward—stumbled, rather—about fifty feet before taking a knee.

After literally and figuratively clearing the dust, I trained my eyes on the horizon. Using memories of satellite imagery that I had studied while planning for our mission, I was looking for landmarks. My entire assault team struggled with the difficult terrain, but managed to sink into the greenery for cover as the helicopter leapt back into the air, where it would meet another Chinook that had dropped off the other half of our assault team about one hundred yards away. Together, the two Chinooks darted off into the distance, and the dust cloud around us finally dissipated.

Silence and darkness set in, and we waited a moment to become silent and dark ourselves. I quickly determined that we weren't dropped off where we had planned, but using a compass attached to my night vision, I set my bearings to a few different rock features I recognized from my map study. Using a small map that was attached to my hip, I plotted my fix on our location before verifying it with a small GPS on my wrist. Once I knew where we were, I started looking around for George.

Our assault team, which was divided into halves, had been ordered to swarm into a village where the Taliban was believed to be operating. What happened next would depend on whether we encountered any hostile fighters.

Based in Afghanistan's southernmost Kandahar Province, our assault team was comprised of both US and Afghan personnel, with most of the American service members being SEALs and the Afghans being Afghan National Army Special Forces (ANASF).

The ANASF commandos we worked with were generally easy to spot, as they were usually loud, a bit clumsy, and unable to effectively conceal themselves. In the dark, they would hiss at each other in Pashto, noisily check their gear, and make an even bigger racket while chambering rounds in their rifles. For whatever reason, they also just couldn't seem to sit still. Navy SEALs, on the other hand, would quickly and quietly blend into their surroundings, and were nearly impossible for a trained officer like me to spot, even with night vision equipment.

After a few moments, George caught my gaze and waved. I pointed out the direction in which I intended to take us, which he confirmed after following the same process that I did. This is how George and I always navigated; we would double-check each other to make sure we didn't wind up getting lost. Even though we sometimes ended up a little bit off course, George and I were always able to navigate our assault team to the right place.

I unfolded my metal detector and switched it on. I waited a moment while it calibrated, then stood and began sweeping the ground for potential IEDs.

During my mission planning, I had researched this area, and was dismayed to see reports of known or suspected IED emplacements popping up all over the map. Due to the prevalence of this hidden threat, our plan was for me or my EOD technician partners, Evan and Leif, to sweep for potential IEDs while the rest of our assault team carefully followed in our footsteps.

We moved this way at all times, with Evan, Leif, and I clearing miles and miles of rugged Afghan terrain. A source of great frustration for the SEALs and ANASF alike, however, was the fact that EOD officers and technicians generally chose difficult, challenging paths to reach our shared objectives. We insisted on this method because the easiest and most appealing course would almost always end up being booby-trapped.

While I was trained and equipped to disable roadside bombs, I would only ever choose to do so if it was absolutely unavoidable. That's because when an EOD officer or technician went "hands on" to render safe an IED, we would be risking our lives, so it was important to ensure that the juice was always worth the squeeze.

Ever since the first American troops set foot in Afghanistan and then Iraq, the enemy's weapon of choice had been the IED. The design and composition of these devices would vary greatly, from simple pressure switches paired with fertilizer-based explosives to optimized shape charges that incorporated military grade explosives, which were usually either stolen or purchased on the black market.

Almost daily, we would receive reports detailing new tactics or IED-related technologies being utilized by insurgents and terrorists. As EOD officers and technicians, it was our job to be well-apprised. It was also our responsibility to identify such hazards while in the field, and then either advise our ground force commander (GFC) on how to best avoid the hazard, or to render it safe, which was most frequently by using our bare hands. That meant Evan, Leif, and I served as our platoon's first line of defense in a battle being waged remotely by cowards hiding in the hills, using buried explosives that didn't discriminate between coalition troops, the women who tended to the fields, or the children who played in them.

Whenever I waved my metal detector back and forth across the ground in front of me, I knew that not only was my own life at stake, but so were the lives of all the men following in my footsteps. With some effort, I was able to put that out of my mind, walk forward, and train my eyes only on my metal detector and the ground. In such a hostile environment, where there is an ever-present list of different things that might kill you at any moment, it's imperative to be able to focus on one thing at a time. George or another SEAL was always right behind me with his rifle up, scanning for potential fighters who might pose a threat to me or the assault team.

Everyone on our assault team had a "field of fire," or an area of responsibility, and each person had knowledge, expertise, or tools that might be needed at any time. All of us were critical to the team, and if any one person failed at their job, someone might die. These are the stakes of combat, and the conditions we faced every time we stepped off the ramp of a Chinook.

Progress was slow, but we patrolled to the edge of the field, then across a small dirt road, and then across another large field. At the edge of the next field, I came to a large irrigation ditch between us and our target building.

"Assault One is preparing for soft breach," said a voice in my left earbud. The voice was that of our GFC, a tall, steely eyed SEAL Lieutenant nicknamed "Fatty," who was actually in great shape.

The other half of our assault team had already reached the target village and was ready to move, which meant that I needed to hurry up. If Assault One breached before we entered the village, we would be at risk of a potential enemy counterattack. At the same time, Assault One was now exposed at the edge of the village. It was important that both teams were ready to begin the assault at the same time, or they could actually pose a hazard to one another.

I used my metal detector to assess the depth of the ditch, realizing that it was more than a few feet deep, and that we wouldn't be able to cross. George then pointed out a small footbridge a few yards to our left, and I shook my head.

"Remember," I said in a quiet voice. "The easiest path is almost always booby-trapped."

"We've got no choice," George whispered. "Assault One has its tail hanging in the breeze!"

Grimacing, I headed toward the footbridge while furiously waving my metal detector. I motioned for George to stay put and get down. If I blew up, I didn't want him or any of the assault team to be hit by fragments from the blast.

With my chest pounding, I carefully scanned the base of the footbridge. Finding nothing, I crept forward while continuing to scan.

Just as I was about to step on the first plank of the bridge, my metal detector started buzzing just to the left of my foot. My eyes widened as I dropped to a knee, carefully placing my metal detector on my right side. I dusted off the spot with my gloved hand and used a small ceramic probe to search the earth around the spot that rang off. Relieved, I quickly unearthed a flattened soup can, and after shaking my head and letting out a quick, nervous laugh, set it aside.

When I resumed my scan, my heartbeat was still the loudest sound I could hear. I made it all the way across the bridge, now content that it was actually clear. I nodded towards George and he made his way to me, with the rest of the team following behind, man by man.

As we traversed a short path to the doorway of our target building, we focused on our objective, which was a one-story house surrounded by a ten-foot mud wall. At the entrance to the compound was a large set of metal doors, hinged on a larger metal frame that had been installed right in the middle of the mud wall.

I cleared past the door to make sure the entrance wasn't booby-trapped, at least from our side, and then used my rifle-mounted laser to sweep the rest of the village in front of me for potential threats.

I could hear George evaluating the metal doors behind me. After some nearly imperceptible tinkering with the door lock, George whispered in my right ear.

"It's locked," he said. "Can you breach this door?"

"Of course," I whispered back with a smile. "I never thought you'd ask."

I began setting up a charge while George handled security. Since we were using explosives, George made sure that Assault One would wait for us to initiate the breach so both teams could begin the assault simultaneously.

After my charge was set, I tapped the back of George's leg and guided him around a nearby corner to shield us from the blast that I was about to set off. While George still had his rifle up, scanning for threats, I squeezed the back of his leg to let him know that I was ready to breach. He called this out over the radio, and when Assault One replied with "standing by," George counted down from three.

When I initiated the breach, we immediately heard the loud snap of C-4 explosives obliterating the door's padlock. Before George could rush forward, the entire metal door frame came loose from the mud wall and toppled forward with a loud crash. Once George saw that the door had fallen, he rushed inside, with the rest of the assault team right on his heels. I cleaned up my breaching equipment before joining them.

In short order, the males in the compound were rounded up, and each room was searched for weapons and possible intelligence. Finding nothing, we continued up the main path of the small village, clearing house by house. Sweeping for IEDs inside the village proved very difficult due to trash, screws, bottle caps, and other littered debris.

About halfway along our intended route, Assault One came over the radio and informed us that they found a suspected cache of homemade explosives. My EOD counterpart on Assault One, Leif, who had temporarily replaced my normal partner Evan on this particular mission, was investigating. So that we wouldn't get too far ahead, Fatty instructed us to stay put until Leif worked through the cache. Through an interpreter, George passed this information on to the Afghan team leader, and directed him to have his commandos take up security positions around the compound we were inside.

As one of the SEALs began working with the interpreter to interview villagers about possible Taliban activity, I told George that I was going to take a quick look around the compound's perimeter. Another SEAL, J.T., then offered to come with me and watch my back.

After exiting the compound on the west side and turning right, I used my metal detector to clear up to the northwest corner of the perimeter wall. As I turned the corner into a small alley running along the north side, J.T. was right behind me with his rifle up. On the left side of the alley, we saw a narrow irrigation ditch, and on the opposing side of the ditch was a mud wall separating us from another farm field to our north.

I froze in my tracks as I looked down the alley. J.T. couldn't see the hair on the back of my neck standing up, but he must have perceived my tension when I stopped in my tracks.

"Whaddya got, man?" J.T. asked.

"Well," I began. "I think I found the mother lode."

Laid out in neat order in front of us were two large rugs, on top of which was a myriad of IEDs, all in different stages of composition. A stack of pressure switches were in one spot and a stack of mortars in another, with a few jugs of fertilizer explosive here and curled up detonating cords there. Somehow, I had managed to find a small IED-making factory.

Upon taking a closer look, J.T. and I gasped when we saw the terrorist's shoes on one edge of one of the rugs. Next to it was a small mug of chai (tea) and a piece of bread on a plate.

"Wow," I said. "This dude was just here!"

Now, every hair on my body was standing, which prompted me to back up a step and take a look around the alley. It was then that I noticed a small, thin wire running from the rugs up into a tree on my left, and then over the farm field wall. Immediately, I thought that there might be an insurgent hiding on the other side of that wall. Quite possibly, he was waiting for us to creep a little bit closer before detonating the bomb that he had left behind.

Quickly and quietly, we backed around the same corner we had come from. J.T. and I then went over everything that we had seen, and after a few moments, I asked him to get on the radio to see if there were any aircraft available. We needed one to take a look at the field to our north and give us a better idea of the immediate threats we were facing.

While J.T. worked that out, I crept back around the corner, using my rifle scope to get another look at the cache of explosives. The morning sun had crawled across the horizon, giving my eyes just enough light to see through the magnifier that I had mounted to my M4 assault rifle. We must have scared off the Taliban insurgent who was making IEDs while eating some breakfast with his morning tea.

As I continued my visual sweep, I noticed something strange in the tree that the wire was running through.

Tucked into a knot in the wood, it appeared as if there was a small cell phone taped to a hand grenade. I had never seen this tactic before, and the need for a cell phone didn't jibe with the wire I had seen running over the wall. Then again, with our lives on the line, I didn't really need to know how exactly this dude was trying to kill us. It was more important to simply realize that he was trying to kill us in the first place.

J.T. tapped me on the shoulder, and let me know that an aircraft took a look at the field to our north and didn't see anyone. Thankfully, that meant no one was on the other end of the suspicious wire.

The cell phone now worried me the most. It didn't really strike me as an active IED, but more likely a device that an insurgent could quickly plant somewhere else. Still, though, I wasn't about to take any unnecessary risks. The most appropriate course of action would be to "blow in place" (BIP) the handheld device. After telling J.T. to stay put, I asked him to let Fatty know that I was going to use a charge to disable an explosive hazard.

I pulled the small explosive charge out of a pouch on my armor, and prepared a short length of time fuse. I told J.T. that it was one minute long, which J.T. quickly relayed to the team. Sweeping the ground with my metal detector, I briskly approached the tree and stuck my charge as close to the hand grenade as possible without actually touching it or the cell phone. I then looked back at J.T., who gave me a "thumbs up," having gotten approval from the GFC to initiate a blast.

I pulled the key ring on the initiator and called "Smoke!" to J.T., who relayed this over the radio. I started a timer on my watch and rushed back around the corner.

"FIRE IN THE HOLE!" I shouted over the radio at the fifty-five second mark.

Again, a loud snap echoed through the otherwise quiet village. This indicated to me that I had gotten the hand grenade to detonate along with my small charge.

When I peeked around the corner, I saw that the entire top of the tree was missing, and was now lying upside down in the irrigation ditch. Much more comforted, yet still wary of potential booby traps, I took my metal detector back out and swept my way up to the IED factory's two rugs.

While J.T. kept an eye out, I pulled out a digital camera and began snapping photos like paparazzi at the Oscars. After thoroughly documenting the scene, I gathered up a few non-hazardous items for forensic investigation after the mission. The pressure switches, for instance, were harmless unless they were added to an initiator and main charge. I grabbed one from a stack and jammed it into my satchel so it could subsequently be analyzed. I also found some pieces of notepaper with Arabic writing, an ID card that I couldn't read, and a small wad of Pakistani money. I stuck it all in the satchel as well.

Now it was time to blow up everything else. I pulled a few explosive charges from my pack and went about setting them up in strategic places in the small factory. I attached a small charge to a stack of mortars, a large jug of fertilizer explosive, and a stack of initiators. I then connected all the charges with detonating cord, looping it around any of the other items left behind by the fleeing insurgent. I kept the detonating cord in place with a few rocks I found nearby, and then attached another one-minute length of time fuse.

I gave a "thumbs up" to J.T., who had been watching from behind the nearby corner. He then called over the radio and directed all stations to prepare for a large detonation. Fatty then came across the radio, acknowledged our notification, and once again gave us permission to proceed.

I pulled the key ring on the time fuse, shouted, "Smoke!" to J.T., and again started my watch. Given that this would be a much bigger explosion, I really booked it back to the nearby corner to take cover.

Just as I called out "FIRE IN THE HOLE!" over the radio, a thunderous explosion leapt out of the ground right behind J.T. and me. Our jaws dropped when we subsequently stood up, looked around the corner, and saw the carnage that had been wrought by the massive explosion.

The enemy IED factory had been destroyed. All that had been neatly arranged on the rugs had been obliterated. Holes were left wherever there had been explosives, while debris from the leveled wall covered everything else. We could now rest assured that no more roadside bombs would be created here for quite some time.

AFTER J.T. REPORTED TO the GFC that the explosion had been successful, we returned to the courtyard just in time for George to tell us that our assault team had to move. Taliban fighters were reportedly headed up from the south, and while our other assault team was tied up with the explosives cache, we needed to provide security in case of an attack.

J.T. volunteered to have my back while I cleared for the patrol, as George would now be very busy coordinating our movements with Assault One. I began clearing south; back in the direction we had originally come from, but also in a different path through the village. Progress was quicker this time as my metal detector found less junk, and there were no more compounds to enter. On our left was a large farm field, while a large cemetery was to our right.

The morning light meant that we no longer needed our night vision equipment, so we flipped our NODs up and out of our field of view. As I paused to do so, I noticed that we were coming up on a T-intersection in the path. I looked back at J.T. and pointed at both of my eyes, then ahead at the intersection. This was our standard signal of a potential hazard being up ahead.

After taking a quick glance at the map on my hip, I told J.T. that this T-intersection was the southernmost path of the village. All that remained were farm fields and eventually desert. The good news was that there weren't many places for the enemy to hide, but at the same time, we would be exposed with little cover. I noted out loud that there was a small building just to the west of the T-intersection, which I thought would be our best chance for cover.

I returned to my sweeping, and just before I came to the intersection, I felt J.T. grasp my armor from behind, which quickly halted my advance.

J.T. had spotted a young man squatting on the path, which was just to our left and toward the building I had spoke of just moments earlier. He hadn't noticed us yet, and was actually staring intently in the other direction, right where our assault teams had originally entered the village.

Behind us, one of the Afghan soldiers shifted uneasily, which caused some of his gear to clang. Startled by the noise, the young man took off running toward the farm fields to the south. As he ran along the wall of the building, J.T. and I both shouted "WADREGA," which means "stop" in Pashto. Despite our demands, the man ran even faster.

Before we could determine whether or not the young man was a threat, he disappeared behind the building to our west.

"Great," J.T. sarcastically muttered.

Having watched the whole series of events unfold, George began feverishly working the radio to see if we could get another aircraft to survey the fields to our south. Was the man running somewhere to inform others of our location? Was he preparing to mount a counterattack of his own? Was he arming himself or other insurgents?

I rapidly swept the intersection while the rest of the assault team filled in around me. Then, one of the SEALs told George that he had a 40mm grenade launcher with CS grenades. A 40mm grenade is egg-sized and can be launched from a small gun—which actually looks a lot like a pirate's blunderbuss—carried by a few members of the assault team. A CS grenade uses a small explosive charge to disperse tear gas. The theory behind such a weapon is that by introducing tear gas, you can ensure that anyone in a given area would evacuate due to extreme discomfort.

By launching a CS grenade in the young man's direction, our hope was that he would then abort his potentially nefarious plan and flee into the open field to our south. It seemed like a great idea at the time, but in the heat of the moment, it never occurred to any of us to check the direction of the wind. When the CS grenade was launched and the SEAL landed a perfect shot just to the left of the corner where the young man had disappeared, the gas began creeping back towards our assault team, much to our collective dismay.

One by one, some of the world's toughest, most highly trained warriors—Navy SEALs, Air Force pararescue jumpers, Afghan Special Forces, a military dog handler, the dog, and a Navy EOD Officer—yours truly—began to cry. I'm not just talking about the watery eyes you might get at the end of *The Notebook*, either. No, these big, tough men began sobbing uncontrollably. One by one, we turned and ran back up the northern path to get as far as possible from the huge cloud of CS gas.

I'd like to say that I was one of the last to give in before running away, but honestly, my eyes were so teary and puffed up, I couldn't see much ahead of me. Quickly, I joined a gaggle of coughing and spitting teammates fifty yards or so up that path we had just come from.

No one spoke as the symptoms of the gas began to subside, but without warning, everyone began to laugh about how ridiculous the whole scene had been. When one of us looked at another's puffy, snot-covered face, we laughed even harder.

"We sure are living up to the 'special' in 'Special Operations' this morning," someone said, which instigated another wave of hearty laughter.

The moment passed, however, and George reminded us that we still needed to move south to protect Assault One. Our situation had just gotten a lot more complicated—if there were indeed fighters coming from the south, they surely knew exactly where we were, thanks to a dissipating cloud of tear gas. After wiping tears and smiles from our faces, we returned to the intersection. We had our rifles up, and despite the tear gas fiasco, we were ready to engage the enemy.

I swept to the building to our west and found a small staircase leading up to its roof. I pointed this out to George and J.T., who both nodded to indicate that I would need to set up a security position on the roof.

Protecting my movement, the SEALs grabbed a few Afghan soldiers and posted them in different shooting positions, establishing as close to a three-hundred-sixty-degree field of fire as possible. I brought one Afghan commando (and his belt-fed machine gun) with me to the roof, which proved to be a perfect firing position.

With such a great vantage point of the fields to our east and south, I identified a field of fire for the commando, who nodded before setting up his weapon to face south by southeast. I flattened myself on the roof, and then started scanning to the east with my rifle. Before I could complete a sweep with my scope from left to right, though, I saw a flash and a puff of white smoke in my peripheral vision. About a second later, I heard a loud boom.

It took me a moment to put the pieces together, but I quickly realized that Taliban fighters had triangulated our position, and were launching mortars at us. I rapidly located the puff of smoke left by the mortar tube, and could just barely make out two fighters hiding in a small clump of trees. I alerted the Afghan commando, and together, we laid down a barrage of gunfire that would have made Arnold Schwarzenegger or Sylvester Stallone jealous. As I dumped an empty magazine and slammed another full one back into my rifle, I heard other members of the assault team come over the radio.

"Was that the BIP from Assault One?" a voice asked over the radio, referring to Leif and the cache of homemade explosives.

"No, no, no!" another voice answered. "We're being mortared!"

"Any casualties?" a different voice asked.

Just a moment of silence after that question sent a chill down my spine. I motioned for the commando to continue firing at the fighters in the trees, while I popped up and ran back down the stairs. When I looked back toward the intersection, I saw nothing but smoke and debris, indicating that the fighters had landed a mortar right on target, at exactly the intersection we had just passed through.

Out of the smoke stumbled a few members of our assault team, who were covered in dust. They appeared to be shell-shocked, but otherwise unharmed.

Among the victims was Shaun, who was a Navy SEAL lieutenant junior grade and our platoon's assistant officer in charge. Shaun told me that Colin, our Air Force pararescue medic, and Dave, our combat photographer, were still back at the intersection.

Fearing the worst, I ran into the smoke cloud, only to find Colin and Dave just like the others: dazed and covered in grayish white dust, but seemingly uninjured. After helping them find their bearings and grab their gear, I ushered them back behind the building to our west.

Upon a more thorough examination, we discovered that Colin had taken shrapnel to his rear end, just next to a tattoo. This discovery—coupled with our collective relief in knowing that he would be okay—sent another wave of laughter through the assault team.

Despite our laughter, however, the miracle that no one had been seriously hurt by the well-aimed mortar fire was not lost on any of us. After getting serious and addressing the needs of the victims, we quickly re-established our security positions, and prepared for another attack.

While we waited, we received confirmation from one of the surveillance aircraft circling above that our barrage of gunfire had killed the two fighters responsible for the mortar attack. Through our interpreter, I passed the news along to the Afghan commando who had shared the rooftop position with me. I was grateful for his help.

After about half an hour, Assault One informed us over the radio that they were ready to blow up the cache of fertilizer that they had found. They would be destroying about five thousand pounds of enemy explosives, which would mark our platoon's biggest cache found during our deployment.

Once we were a safe distance from what promised to be a huge blast, my EOD partner on this busy day, Leif, shouted "FIRE IN THE HOLE!" over the radio just before his five-minute time fuse ran out.

The ensuing blast truly felt like an earthquake. I looked to our northwest, where Assault One had previously been located, and saw a large, gray mushroom cloud reaching up into the clear blue sky. Our collective jaws dropped before all of us began shouting in unison.

"HELL YEAH!" we screamed.

13

Becoming a Warrior

My deployment to Afghanistan quickly settled into a regular, almost comforting rhythm. My team would go out on a mission just about every four or five days before returning to our small station near Kandahar Airfield. The day after each mission, we would rest and discuss what went right, what went wrong, and how we could do better next time.

For the next couple of days after a mission, I would wake up early for a big breakfast before working out in the gym for about two hours. Then, I would spend a few hours in the tactical operations center (TOC) reviewing e-mails and reports from war-torn Afghanistan. After lunch, I would return to the TOC to work on research for our next mission before heading back to the gym for another workout. I'd grab a large dinner, clean up, watch a movie or two, and then head off to bed. I actually loved having such a regular routine, even though I was technically in a war zone.

My life in Afghanistan was simple: we had a purpose, and most of each day was dedicated to fulfilling it. While the gravity and risk associated with our tasks were often immense, we were increasingly able to turn our figurative combat switch on and off, and our rhythm helped very much to facilitate that balance.

We didn't have smart phones with us and the Internet was frustratingly slow, so when not out on a mission, we occupied ourselves otherwise. It's amazing how much free time you discover when you don't spend most of your life on Facebook and Twitter.

One morning in Afghanistan, I logged into my e-mail after a good workout and found an update from my EOD command back home about my DUI. I had previously received a letter of reprimand from the Navy, which prescribed no further punitive measures. Still, it would serve as a record of the incident and be considered by any future promotional boards. This would certainly harm my chances at advancement, but again, nothing in the letter of reprimand had seemed to threaten my immediate future in the Navy.

This particular e-mail update, however, was about an aspect of the process that I had failed to recognize. According to Navy regulations, all letters of reprimand filed for officers had to be reviewed by a flag officer, which went from the rank of rear admiral all the way up to four-star admiral. As I served in Afghanistan, it turned out that my letter of reprimand had indeed worked its way up the chain of command all the way to an admiral's desk.

Upon review of my letter, the admiral ruled that alcohol-related incidents—especially those involving DUIs or other criminal charges—would not be tolerated. Apparently, he was particularly determined to institute a zero tolerance-type policy for officers, since we were supposed to set an example for other sailors at all times. Therefore, the admiral recommended that I be separated from naval service.

In an instant, I realized that while I went about my daily duties half a world away, the process to kick me out of the military was already well underway on the home front.

An attached letter from the Navy's personnel bureau presented me with two choices. I could either accept a general—not honorable—discharge from the Navy, or I could appeal the admiral's decision.

Even though my horrendous mistake was never far from my thoughts, being in a combat zone hadn't exactly given me much of an opportunity to sit down and think about my future. But as I stared at an e-mail outlining my mandatory separation from the Navy, my future began to look extremely bleak.

My EOD command, which had advocated on my behalf to let me deploy, initiated my formal appeal to the admiral's tough decision. Since I was in a war zone, my command also assured me that they would handle the process on my behalf. They implored me to focus on my mission and my platoon.

Even though I wasn't really sure what to think, I had no choice but to do exactly what I was told. The stakes in Afghanistan were too high to spend one more second thinking about myself instead of the men I was responsible for leading in combat.

A FEW DAYS LATER, everyone woke up just a little earlier than usual. Our platoon went to breakfast together, but didn't say much to one another while polishing off an extravagant amount of food. As usual, we then put away our empty trays and walked back to our barracks compound. After each of us showered, shaved, and put on a clean uniform, we piled into our platoon's three Toyota 4Runners to make the short drive to Kandahar Airfield.

We parked at the edge of a long runway, where a C-17 waited nearby with its ramp down. An Army corporal then ushered us over to join a few dozen Army Special Forces soldiers before directing us to a path that led to the ramp of the massive aircraft. The morning was still, and aside from the sound of a gentle breeze flowing across the vast airstrip, there was not much to be heard.

After a few moments, we were called to attention as a solemn procession began to move between our ranks. Before we could blink, a group of sharply dressed US Army personnel was quietly surrounding and lifting a large casket with an American flag draped over the top.

Inside the casket was a senior team leader who had been killed not far from a location where we had found the cache of IEDs and explosives a few days earlier. The man had dedicated nearly twenty years of his life to the Army, with most of that time spent as a Special Forces operator. He had made numerous deployments to both Iraq and Afghanistan, and now, he would return to American soil for the last time.

The procession moved in front of me, and from somewhere in the ranks, I could hear an American soldier choking back a sob. Slowly, the procession reached the ramp of the aircraft, where the casket was gently loaded and tied down. The Army detail then left the aircraft and marched back to the edge of the airstrip. The ramp was raised, which prompted the aircraft to spin around, taxi for a short distance, fire up its engines, and then lift off.

When that same ramp eventually lowered at Dover Air Force Base in Delaware, the fallen warrior's wife and two children would be waiting in tears. While thinking about the sacrifices of that grieving widow, along with two kids who would now be forced to grow up without a father, tears of my own began to fall from my suddenly trembling eyes.

In that profound moment, I resolved that I would do everything in my power to ensure that none of the men in my platoon would return to their loved ones inside flag-draped caskets. To all of us who witnessed the Army's solemn farewell to a true American hero, the stakes of our mission in Afghanistan had never been clearer. In silence, we piled back into the 4Runners and returned to our base.

THE GIANT ENGINES OF a Chinook helicopter roared above me as the rotors made deep "thump, thump, thump" sounds. While engulfed by the night's shadows, I had temporarily allowed my thoughts to drift to one of my favorite childhood beaches before feeling a nudge that jerked me back to reality. The nudge was from the muzzled snout of our multi-purpose canine (MPC), which was a large German Shepherd dog named Max.

I would have liked to think that Max was trying to tell me that we were landing, but in reality, he was probably making a desperate plea for me to remove his muzzle, which absolutely needed to be on since Max was a trained attack dog. Still, I reached down and gave Max a scratch behind the ears. Even though my words were lost in the rotor wash, I apologized to the dog for having to endure such a difficult ride.

As my eyes peered out over the edge of the ramp, I saw that our assault team's two helicopters were rushing through another valley surrounded by large, harsh-looking mountains. The landscape at the base of the valley was vastly different from the lush grape fields from our previous mission. This time, all I could see was barren, dry desert. With no apparent decrease in forward velocity, the helicopter dropped suddenly, and quickly lost altitude.

After a moment of terror, I realized that this was a deliberate maneuver by our expert pilots to avoid potential enemy fire, and that instead of crashing, we were about to set down and dismount. The ground's dust was kicked up by the rotor wash as our choppers approached, and almost immediately, we were engulfed in a huge dust cloud.

For a moment, I closed my dusty eyes and focused on the feel of the chopper lowering. I sensed the rear of the aircraft sink lower than the front, which was consistent with the way a helicopter should land.

After an abrupt bump, which I assumed came from the Chinook's wheels hitting the ground, I unclipped and stood up, ready to run off the helicopter as soon as the ramp began to lower. The only problem was that the ramp did not go down. Instead, the entire helicopter abruptly leapt back into the air, which almost sent me over the lip of the ramp and out of the aircraft.

In a split second, I threw my weight back down and flattened myself against the ramp. I caught my balance just in time to feel the aircraft sharply drop again. This time, I waited until I was sure that I felt the ramp moving, and when I did, I jumped up as quickly as I could and took off running.

The barren desert floor was much easier to adjust to than the farm fields from the previous mission. After sprinting fifty yards out of the ramp and settling down on one knee to check my gear, I began getting my bearings and scanning for threats.

When I glanced back for a moment, I was shocked to find that I couldn't see more than a few feet back toward the helicopter. In fact, I couldn't see the Chinook at all, nor could I see anyone else from our assault team. I could faintly make out an eerie halo of green static electricity, which was caused by dust particles striking and rubbing the large rotors of the aircraft, and was only visible because of my NODs. I grinned slightly as I became amused by this small miracle of science.

It also occurred to me that the big bump that had almost thrown me out of the helicopter must have been the pilot second-guessing his landing, which was perfectly understandable since the ground had become quickly and completely occluded by the giant dust cloud. It was amazing—and very scary—to consider how quickly things can get chaotic and potentially go awry once I lost my ability to see.

Thankful to be alive, I turned my attention forward and scanned the faint horizon with my compass to try to get a handle on our exact location. Just as swiftly as they had come down, minus the terrifying moment that almost sent me flying into the southern Afghanistan desert, the helicopters jumped back up into the air, leaned forward, and flew away.

As the dust settled and the thumping Chinook rotors faded into the night, our platoon was suddenly surrounded by sand, mountains, and silence. After getting as oriented as I could to the uncommon setting, I charted a course to the south. Upon receiving a nod from my team leader, a different SEAL named Ray, I pulled out my trusty metal detector and began sweeping.

We had to hike through the desert for about four miles before we would reach a target village, where we believed the Taliban was operating. My platoon's mission, once again, was to work with Afghan commandos to penetrate and secure the village. While I had read intelligence reports about the area, I didn't know if we would be greeted by Taliban gunfire or sleeping Afghan villagers. As always, I had no choice but to prepare for the worst.

Thankfully, there was little terrain to negotiate, as it was uncommon for the enemy to randomly place IEDs in the middle of a large desert. Considering this tendency, I believed we were in for a pleasant early morning hike. That is, as pleasant as a hike can be in the middle of a desert in Afghanistan while carrying sixty pounds of gear and armor, all while Taliban fighters hide in the mountains wanting to kill everyone in your group.

I sought out large rocks and dried-out riverbeds for as much cover as I could find, and soon, the cool night desert began to feel much warmer due to our increasing exertion. Every fifteen minutes or so, I stopped to glance back at our patrol to make sure everyone was still able to follow the path that I had cleared.

No matter how often I would adjust, and regardless of how much effort I had put into slimming down my load, it never took long for my armor and gear to feel uncomfortable and cumbersome. My helmet would start to feel heavy, my armor would pull down on my neck and shoulders, and my pack and rifle sling would seem to rub long cuts into my neck. After a while, though, I just had to learn to be comfortable being uncomfortable.

After about an hour or so of hiking, I saw a shape on the horizon that didn't match the desert or mountains. It had unnatural square angles forming a rectangle, and was clearly manmade. I stopped for a moment to check my map as Ray crept up behind me. I felt him approach, and without looking up, I whispered what I had seen into his ear. Then, using a small, red LED light, I pointed out where I thought we were on my map. Ray referred to his compass and map for a moment, and then agreed with my assessment.

I took a quick sip of water before resuming my sweep, which took our patrol as close as possible to the mountains on the west side of the valley. My goal was to get us as much cover and concealment as possible during our approach to the village.

It had been a while since the Chinooks left, and our patrol had remained relatively silent ever since. Hopefully, no one in the village would suspect our approach. Inevitably, though, a dog would probably catch our scent in the breeze and start barking. The closer we got, the faster we would need to move.

Slowly, the rectangle on the horizon grew and grew until I could see that it was a small building with an adjoining yard, which was surrounded by a low wall. As we got closer, I was able to see the outlines of more buildings just beyond. At about half a mile away, I found a small area where our assault team could gather for a minute. At this point, it was our plan for half the assault to break away, follow a dried-up riverbed just to the east, and make entry into the village at a different point. Then, both assault teams would clear through the village in parallel and we would work our way south, with the GFC coordinating our efforts using satellite technology.

While studying the village and wolfing down a breakfast bar, I was pleased to discover that nobody appeared to be moving. Thankfully, there was still no sign that anyone suspected our oncoming raid. In fact, I could faintly make out the figures of what appeared to be villagers sleeping atop the roofs of their mud-walled homes.

As anticipated, though, a dog began to bark. The villagers still probably didn't suspect an attack, but we sure as heck weren't going to wait around for them to think about it much longer. Moments later, the GFC's voice crackled over the radio, giving us the go-ahead for the assault to begin.

The last half-mile was relatively wide open, so I led us toward the village in as close to a sprint as I could manage while sweeping for explosives and trying to keep quiet. I quickly reached a wall near the northernmost compound, and waited a moment as the rest of the assault team fell in line behind me. The wall was about eight feet high, so I would need to use one of our foldable ladders to climb up onto the roof before clearing a way into the compound.

Somehow, I had to climb up the ladder and use my metal detector to sweep the roof for Taliban booby traps without waking the sleeping villagers. Of course, I would also need to have my weapon ready in case one of the villagers woke up and grabbed his AK-47.

I slung my rifle to my side before pulling out my pistol and a smaller, wand-like metal detector that I kept in my armor vest. At the same time, Ray and one of the Afghan commandos worked to unfold the ladder.

When the commando positioned the ladder on the side of the building, however, he abruptly set it down, resulting in a large thud. I waited a moment to see if the crashing sound had alerted the sleeping villagers, but thankfully, I heard no movement. Ray and I glared at the Afghan soldier, who responded with an apologetic look.

The hair on the back of my neck stood up as I started going up the ladder without much cover. I peered over the top, and saw one man sleeping only a few feet away. Luckily, he had somehow slept through the sound of the crashing ladder and there was no one else around him. The man wasn't sleeping with a sheet or blanket that might conceal a rifle, and I didn't see any weapons in the vicinity. In all likelihood, this man was a villager rather than a Taliban insurgent. I also doubted that he would knowingly sleep next to an IED planted on the roof. While responsible for other men's lives, though, I couldn't afford to take any risks.

Without taking my eyes off the sleeping man, I quietly and carefully pulled myself up onto the roof. As soon as I was clear of the ladder, I swiftly moved over to the sleeping man, put my hand over his mouth, and shook him awake. He was obviously startled, and I could see his eyes open wide through my night vision goggles. I must have looked like some sort of demon from the future to him, especially since the only thing visible to him would be small, green night vision halos around my eyes.

For a moment, my adrenaline spiked even higher than it had been as I crept up the ladder. I stood up, ushered the man to do the same, and pointed towards a stairway that led down from the roof into the compound's courtyard. Without a moment of hesitation, the man acquiesced and began to move towards the stairway. Over my radio, I whispered to Ray that the roof was clear, which prompted him to immediately rush up the ladder. A few Afghan commandos followed as I urged the man down the stairway and into the courtyard.

At the base of the stairs, I peered into the courtyard, and was pleased to find that the man's wife and children were apparently sleeping outside on mats in the middle of the courtyard. Even if this man was a Taliban fighter, which I doubted by this point, it would make no sense for him to booby trap the home that his family was sleeping in. Confident that no one would step on an IED, I glanced back up the staircase and motioned to Ray that we could let the other Afghan commandos loose in the compound. Ray nodded and whispered back to an interpreter, who was standing on the stairway just behind him.

From the base of the stairs, I watched as the commandos rushed in and began clearing the compound. They went over to the man's sleeping family, woke them up, and put them in one corner of the courtyard. They brought the man who had been sleeping on the roof over to another corner to begin asking him questions. Other commandos ran through every room in the small home, and came out shaking their heads after a few minutes, which indicated that they didn't find anything of interest.

When Ray checked with the interpreter and the group interrogating the man, his story matched my hunch. As it turned out, he was just a simple Afghan farmer managing a few fields in the surrounding area. Our approach had been across barren desert, but this village did have a few bright green poppy fields surrounding a few of its mud buildings. I had little doubt that the man was telling the truth about his occupation.

When it came to our next question, however, I wasn't so sure about his candor. We asked the man if he had seen any Taliban during the last few days, and he emphatically shook his head to indicate that he hadn't. In all likelihood, he was lying, probably because he was required to sell his poppy to the Taliban. If he didn't, he would almost certainly have been beaten, tortured, or even killed. He would have faced a similarly brutal fate if the Taliban even suspected that he had cooperated with foreign troops.

Intelligence reports led us to strongly believe that the Taliban was indeed operating in the area, and specifically this particular village. After wrapping up our interview with the man, we moved from compound to compound, finding more apparent villagers and their families. Most of the military-age males we questioned said the same thing: they were farmers who knew nothing about the Taliban or where they might be operating.

After peering into room after room without seeing any indication of Taliban activity, I began to believe these men. Just as that thought popped into my head, though, a loud voice crackled over the radio requesting that I come to "Building Thirty-Eight." Had they found a group of Taliban fighters? Or maybe even an IED? My heart and mind began to race.

I looked at Ray, who had heard the same thing over his radio. As he checked over his map, Ray pointed out that there were still a few buildings to clear between us and Building Thirty-Eight. He said that if there were Taliban fighters hiding in any of those buildings, they would most likely pose a greater threat than whatever we would find inside Building Thirty-Eight.

I agreed, and asked Alaska, the SEAL on the other end of the radio, if there were any suspected Taliban fighters in the building. Alaska said he didn't think so, but at the same time, he hadn't been able to clear the building because he had found a suspected IED hidden in the doorframe. My heart and mind began racing even faster.

After five years as an EOD officer, I still hadn't stared down a "ready to explode" enemy bomb, even though I had gotten very close with that IED factory and explosives cache we had found on a previous mission. In reality, though, I believed that nothing I blew up in the alley that day had been an active roadside bomb, but only pieces and parts.

If Alaska had in fact found a real IED, this would be my day of reckoning. It would be my first opportunity to validate my place on the assault team and put my training to the test, as well as, for lack of a better term, my nuts. Did I have what it took to disable a Taliban bomb with my bare hands?

As my heart leapt into my throat, Ray instructed Alaska to grab a secure position and keep eyes on Building Thirty-Eight while we cleared everything in between. We found nothing, and after about fifteen minutes, Ray led us to a large, two-story compound only a few hundred yards away from Building Thirty-Eight before direct-ing the Afghan commandos to set up a security perimeter. Ray then said he would come with me to meet Alaska, who was hunkered down in a small group of trees along an irrigation ditch near Build-ing Thirty-Eight, along with another SEAL named Red.

Building Thirty-Eight was a mud-walled hut that couldn't have been more than thirty feet long and twelve feet wide. It was tall, however, standing about sixteen feet high on a crest at the south-ernmost point of the village. The building also offered a great van-tage point for the valley to our south. It made sense that this building might be booby-trapped, as the Taliban might have pre-dicted that if American troops were to assault the village, we might do so from the south. Under that scenario, Building Thirty-Eight would have been the first we would encounter. When the IED blew up, it would not only have killed several of us, but alerted the Tali-ban to our presence.

Ray offered to help Red provide overwatch while Alaska guided me to the doorway where he explained that he had seen the tail of a mortar sticking out of the ground. Mortar tails were actually not un-common to see in war-torn Afghan villages, as the remnants of ex-ploded or unexploded ordnance were all over. For a moment, I thought that Alaska might have simply seen a mortar tail that some-one was using for a doorstop (yes, that was actually possible!), and that my chance to disable a real IED would have to wait.

When I asked Alaska to describe how the mortar tail had been sticking out of the ground, he clarified that it wasn't only the tail, but a full mortar round buried just in front of the doorway. Now I was sure it was, in fact, an IED.

"It's gigantic," Alaska said of the mortar.

Mortars are identified by their diameter, with 80mm—a little larger than a baseball on one end, with a tail on the other—being the most common. Alaska estimated that this mortar round, however, was 105mm, which was about the size of an NFL football. I figured that gave it a net explosive weight of about twenty pounds, which would likely kill a person who stepped on it, while maiming the person(s) standing behind.

Upon this realization, my heart seemed to beat just as loudly as Alaska's voice. My moment had finally arrived, and I couldn't have been any more nervous.

As I followed Alaska along a narrow path leading up the embankment and around to the front of the building, my mind's eye ran through all I had seen in recent IED reports. This device was most likely a pressure plate, which was most common. But what if it was something else? Could it have been a remote-fired device, which a Taliban fighter was waiting to trigger from a vantage point we had missed inside the village, or perhaps even a nearby mountain? These types of dreadful scenarios filled my head as we approached Building Thirty-Eight.

Before my imagination could run too wild, we reached the back of the building. I told Alaska to stand back, but also to keep an eye on me, as well as the valley to our south. The sun was coming up now, and my movements would be obvious to anyone watching from the mountains on either side or from the valley to the south. I doubted anyone was there, but at the same time, I wanted someone who I could trust watching my back.

I pulled out my large metal detector and began clearing a path around to the front of the building, while being careful to stay away from its walls, which was exactly where I would have placed secondary explosives if I had been a bad guy.

As soon as my eyes reached the front of the building, I saw the mortar tail that Alaska had identified. Keeping my distance, I kept sweeping in an arc with my metal detector around to the front of the building so I could get a better look at the device.

Alaska was spot on. The mortar was mostly buried, but I could see a portion of the wide explosive end. Alaska's assessment that it was a 105mm mortar was almost certainly correct.

Upon first glance, I didn't see any apparent initiation system. As my sweat began to drip, I slowly crept forward towards the IED while perpetually scanning the immediate area around Building Thirty-Eight. Then, I glanced toward the mountains and the valley, which were now behind me.

When I got within about six feet of the device, I saw something that froze me in my tracks. A small, thin wire was protruding from the sand where the nose of the mortar should have been. The wire ran up a foot or two to the door frame on the right side of the door before disappearing into the shadows beyond the doorway.

A couple thoughts went through my already racing mind. Either the wire ran to a handheld detonator that someone was holding inside, or to a detonator that could be triggered by a cell phone. Facing possible death, I had to make a snap decision.

I quickly opted for a BIP, which wasn't exactly "hands on," but still counted in my book. I would remove one of the small charges that I kept in my chest rig, place it on the exposed part of the mortar, and then try to blow it up after I took cover.

Sometimes, EOD technicians would avoid this tactic if we needed to preserve the immediate area. But during this tense moment, the last thing I cared about was the future of a small, mud building. Most importantly, a BIP was the safest method to ensure the safety of both myself and my assault team.

I pulled out my charge and showed it to Alaska, who knew exactly what my intentions were. Over the radio, he told the GFC that I intended to blow up the device. As he spoke, I quickly calculated that the ensuing blast would only go about ten feet into the air. Since the IED was facing south and the rest of my team was to the north, they would be protected from blast fragments originating from Building Thirty-Eight.

With my plan set, I quickly moved over top of the mortar. This was the moment of greatest risk, but strangely, I had stopped feeling nervous. My heartbeat was now steady, my breathing was smooth, and my profuse sweating had subsided. I was calm and completely in the moment. I was doing what I had been trained to do.

Not wasting any time, I placed a small amount of plastic explosive on the exposed mortar and carefully laid out a minute's worth of fuse. I took one last look at the mortar and the thin wire before pulling the small key ring initiator at the end of the time fuse. Upon confirming that the fuse had lit, I called "Smoke!" to Alaska, who passed this along on the radio. Swiftly but carefully, I stood up, backed away, and then retraced my steps around the building. After reaching Alaska, we bounded down the embankment together.

"FIRE IN THE HOLE!" I shouted over the radio at the fifty-five second mark.

Barely one second later, a crack and a loud "BOOM" echoed through the previously quiet southern Afghanistan valley. I must have started my watch late, but I was close enough. The mortar had exploded.

Alaska and I grinned at each other before darting up the embankment. When we reached our previous position, Alaska held up

This picture of me was taken while my family lived in Reno, Nevada.

My father, Michael, was the first person to introduce me to the water.

My brother Mitchell, right, helped me dream of becoming a real-life G.I. Joe.

Mitchell, left, and my brother Russell, right, loved our backyard pool in Bradenton, Florida. For the Snyders, swimming was always a family affair.

This is a family portrait of Russell, me, Mitchell, and our baby sister, Elyse.

Inspired by the stories of our grandparents, my siblings and I decided to dress up in makeshift military uniforms.

This photo shows Elyse and me in our favorite place: the water.

My family was excited to visit Annapolis after I completed "plebe summer" at the US Naval Academy. My mother, Valarie, is on the right.

Visiting my family home in St. Petersburg, Florida, was a welcome respite during my Naval Academy days.

I know this Naval Academy portrait was taken after plebe year since my hair had grown back.

This photo was taken during another visit home to St. Petersburg.

This is my cheesy "thumbs up" after disabling my first active enemy IED in Afghanistan.

During my deployment to Afghanistan, I spent a lot of time with our multi-purpose canine, Max.

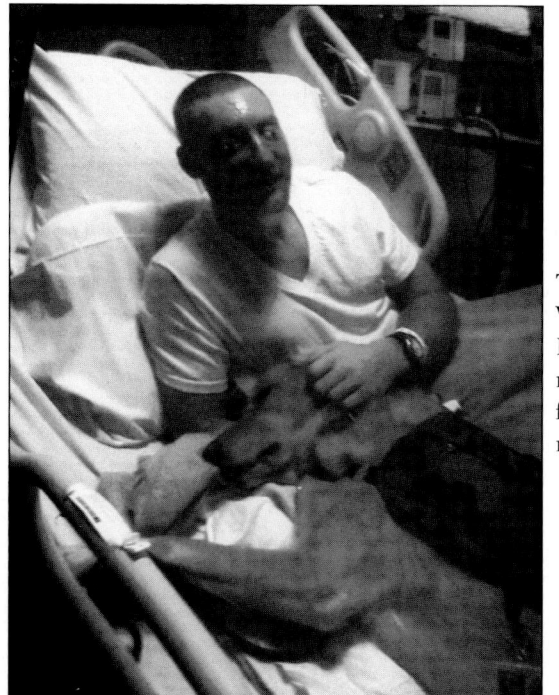

The service dogs at the Walter Reed National Military Center gave me comfort during the first few weeks after my injury.

My coach, Brian Loeffler, helped navigate me back into the pool. *Courtesy: US Air Force/Master Sergeant Sean M. Worrell.*

This photo was taken while I was training for the 2012 Paralympic Games.

I will never forget walking out to the pool with Brian on my first Alive Day—September 7, 2012—for the biggest race of my life: the 400m freestyle at the 2012 Paralympic Games in London.

A fist pump felt appropriate after Brian told me I won.

Receiving the gold medal is a moment I will never forget.

While singing along with "The Star-Spangled Banner" on the podium in London, I thought of the many people who helped me arrive at this improbable moment.

After the ceremony, I made sure to thank the wonderful crowd in London.

I met Defense Secretary Leon Panetta at the Pentagon on September 13, 2012, with fellow Paralympians Kari Miller, Jeremy Campbell, and Cortney Jordan. *Courtesy: US Navy/Petty Officer First Class Chad McNeeley.*

It was an incredible honor to present the American flag to President Barack Obama, first lady Michelle Obama, and Vice President Joe Biden with US Olympic fencer Mariel Zagunis at the White House on September 14, 2012. *Courtesy: US Air Force/ Desiree N. Palacios.*

After the ceremony, I thanked the first lady for sharing my story in a recent speech. *Courtesy: The White House.*

It was thrilling to return to Annapolis for the Navy-San Jose State football game on September 29, 2012, for an on-field ceremony with US Navy Admiral Jonathan Greenert, Secretary of the Navy Ray Mabus, Vice Admiral Michael H. Miller, Navy Athletic Director Chet Gladchuk, Navy men's swimming coach Bill Roberts, and Lieutenant Jake Keefe. *Courtesy: US Navy/Mass Communication Specialist First Class Peter D. Lawlor.*

Delivering the keynote address at the Navy-Marine Corps Ball in Washington on March 23, 2013, inspired me to continue sharing my story through public speaking. *Courtesy: US Navy/Mass Communication Specialist First Class Peter D. Lawlor.*

At the 2012 Warrior Games in Colorado Springs, I thanked US Army Captain Ivan Castro for helping put my new life into perspective. *Courtesy: US Special Operations Command/Technical Sergeant Heather Kelly.*

I returned to Colorado Springs on May 11, 2013, to light the Warrior Games torch with US Olympic swimmer and gold medalist Missy Franklin and Prince Harry. *Courtesy: US Marine Corps/Lance Corporal Scott Reel.*

I enjoyed visiting Alaska in 2014 with my family, my guide dog, Gizzy, and family friends Nancy and Ross Sarratt.

My family visited Springfield, Missouri, in November 2015 to celebrate the induction of my brother, Mitchell, left, to Drury University's Athletic of Hall of Fame for his accomplishments as a collegiate swimmer.

Gizzy and I now call Baltimore home. *Courtesy: Under Armour.*

The opening ceremony for the 2016 Paralympic Games will be held in Rio de Janeiro, Brazil, on September 7: my fifth Alive Day. *Courtesy: US Olympic Committee.*

his rifle and scanned for threats while I swept back up to the front of the building. To my elation, the mortar had indeed blown up, and taken a good chunk of the building's front side with it. If there had been anyone inside, they would either be dead or incapacitated by the blast.

After determining that no one had been inside Building Thirty-Eight, I asked Alaska to join me in checking out the damage. Alaska smiled as he turned the corner and saw what I had done. He then pulled out his camera and told me to pose. As he snapped the picture, I threw up a cheesy "thumbs up" sign, which was the first thing that came to mind. Alaska then slapped my back and congratulated me on disabling my first active enemy IED. It was a truly remarkable feeling.

BY THE TIME THE sun went down that evening, we had patrolled up a mountain to the west of the village. Once up on the plateau, our assault team dug in and hid. At around midnight, two Chinook helicopters swooped in, but instead of boarding them, we just took off supplies of water and food. Our intention was to trick possible enemy fighters into thinking that we had left the area after clearing the village. In many cases, the Taliban would re-enter these villages after thinking the Americans were gone.

For the rest of the night, a few of the SEALs and I took turns watching over the village, while the rest of the team attempted to get a few hours of rest. From about 2 a.m. to 4 a.m., I would team up with a SEAL we nicknamed "Sarge" since he had been a Marine sergeant before transitioning to the Navy and eventually BUD/S training.

At first, Sarge and I watched in silence as I used my night vision and a small thermal imager to scan for fighters who might have been hiding in nearby mountains or the valley below.

That's when Sarge and I both noticed a strange blinking light in the distance. Then, from a different direction, another light blinked, seemingly in response. After watching this exchange for a few moments, we concluded that two fighters were communicating through some type of Taliban Morse code. Unable to figure out what they were saying, Sarge and I just watched, hoping that the fighters would move back into the village so that we could capture them the next morning.

After about an hour of watching the blinking lights, the initial excitement of our discovery had worn off. To combat the ensuing wave of exhaustion, Sarge and I began to talk. After swapping a few funny training stories, we somehow wandered into a deep discussion about how we had both ended up in the desolate, treacherous mountains of Afghanistan.

As the Navy SEAL and I reflected on our shared commitment to serve, I recalled sitting in my backyard in Colorado Springs when I was eight years old. I thought about playing with those G.I. Joes and hoping that someday, I would become a warrior.

I then recalled the events of that very morning, and smiled at the thought of blowing up that enemy IED. At the same time, my peripheral vision caught the American flag patch on my armor, along with my slung rifle.

In that special moment under the starry sky, I wished that the eight-year-old Brad Snyder could have met twenty-seven-year-old Brad. I firmly believed that eight-year-old Brad would have been a pretty big fan of his twenty-seven-year-old counterpart. This humorous comparison made me smile, and a feeling of strong connection to my purpose washed over me.

Finally, I had become what I had always wanted to become. I was a real-life G.I. Joe, trained to defend my country at any cost. I had become a warrior.

14

The Night Osama bin Laden Was Killed

Before the sun poked above the horizon, we had moved back into the village, but we found nothing different from the day before. While we could hear the Taliban anxiously chattering on the radio about assembling a possible attack on our forces, it never happened. The sun set once more, and after a few hours, the Chinooks landed in the valley just to our south to give us a ride back to base.

The Chinooks dropped us off at the helicopter pad near the Afghan commandos' compound. Exhausted, sweaty, smelly, achy, hungry, and thirsty, we ambled off the helicopters only to learn that we were going to have to walk the rest of the way. It was a mile and a half from the Afghan helicopter pad to our base, and most importantly, our showers and comfy beds.

The last mile and a half shouldn't have been that big a deal. But after forty-eight hours of hiking through the Afghan mountains, it might as well have been one hundred fifty miles. When I looked at the men of my platoon, I could see in their eyes that everyone felt just like I did. But after a brief moment of self-pity, we uttered a collective, cynical "roger that" and began to hike home with stoic faces. On the surface, it was a small, relatively insignificant moment. To me, it demonstrated the unbreakable will of my platoon.

The hike started in silence, but as we got closer to our compound, our voices picked up and the jokes started to fly. There was a feeling of elation and relief as we passed through the gates to our home away from home, and quickly, the stoicism on our faces was replaced by ear-to-ear grins. We filed into our barracks building, and in unison, began stripping off our heavy gear. The collective funk aggregated in a way that no Yankee Candle could cover up, but we didn't care. We were "home."

I unloaded my rifle and pistol and set them inside my room. Next, I ran across the compound to remove my explosives in a safe holding area that the team maintained a distance away from where we slept.

When I went back to the barracks, I felt lighter and quicker just from offloading that relatively small amount of gear. As I sat down on a small bench in front of my room to peel off my boots, a member of my platoon shouted five incredible words, which echoed through the hallway.

"They killed Osama bin Laden!" one of my teammates yelled.

What? Did he just say what I think he said?

I had so many questions, but could it be? Not that I would have been privy to such sensitive, top secret information, but no one I had ever worked with, including the SEALs in my platoon, had ever hinted at having the slightest idea of bin Laden's location. Even though I was in Afghanistan, I suppose that I subscribed to the same conventional wisdom as the rest of the world in 2011: Osama bin Laden was probably in Pakistan, but the trail had gone cold.

I ripped off my boots, threw the rest of my armor in a pile, and rushed toward a computer. We were fortunate to have Internet at all, but still, it was incredibly frustrating to watch the little spinning pinwheel indicating that the URL bar was still loading. As we continued to wait, it seemed like every US service member stationed in Afghanistan was typing "Osama bin Laden" into their search bars at the exact same time.

Finally, the pinwheel disappeared, and a headline from CNN appeared. It confirmed bin Laden's death.

The members of my platoon and I were shocked upon learning that the 9/11 ringleader had been found in Abbottabad, Pakistan, which wasn't that far from our location in Afghanistan. Sometime during the previous night, while Sarge and I had watched Taliban fighters communicating from a mountaintop with blinking lights, members of a different SEAL team had boarded Black Hawk helicopters and stormed a small compound across the border. One or more of those SEALs, we assumed, had shot and killed the man responsible for the deaths of thousands of innocent Americans.

I sat back in amazement at first, not really knowing what to make of this news. I recalled sitting in Mrs. Archer's class as a seventeen-year-old high school senior and watching in horror on our classroom television set as the second plane hit the World Trade Center. Like so many others, I knew the rest of my life would be different after that terrible moment. Now, almost ten years later, here I was sitting in a filthy combat uniform in desolate southern Afghanistan, with my eyes once again staring at momentous news on a small screen. I felt like the last decade of my life had truly come full circle.

Deep down, I knew that the death of one man wasn't going to solve anything substantial. I knew that I would remain deployed, along with thousands of men and women like me. I knew that there would be more terrorist plots, and that we would still be asked to disrupt them. I knew that despite our best efforts, more Americans, Afghans, Iraqis, and people of other nationalities would almost certainly die during the ongoing war on terror.

Despite these stark realizations, I still felt an overwhelming sense of triumph. I may not have been in Abbottabad for the raid on bin Laden's compound, but I was only a few hundred miles away. Sure, I was on a different mission in a different country with a different platoon. But on that historic night, we all had the same goal as the heroes who had been on that raid. We wanted to make the world a better place. Therefore, I firmly believed that I was in the right place with the right men, doing the right thing.

ONE WEEK LATER, an abrupt knock on the door penetrated the pitch black of my small barracks room, which jerked me from a deep slumber. After a moment of confusion, I realized that the knock had occurred in real life, rather than a dream. Before I could move, the knock repeated, sounding louder and harsher. I bolted upright, moved to the door, and ripped it open, becoming temporarily blinded by the hallway's bright lights.

My boss, the SEAL lieutenant nicknamed Fatty, was standing in my doorframe, appearing as a dark silhouette against the hall's fluorescent light. Ignoring how close he got to me, he stepped inside, and was obviously uncomfortable.

"Brad, there's no easy way to tell you this…" he blurted out.

Oh, no … I thought.

Fatty wouldn't knock on my door this late unless it was bad … real bad. Had a member of my platoon been killed? Their names raced through my mind as I tried to recall the last time I had spoken to each one. Where were they? What were they doing?

I concluded that one or more of my teammates must have been dead. That was why Fatty was in my room in the middle of the night. Next, my panicked thoughts shifted to how the tragedy had occurred. Was it an IED or a shooting? I immediately felt sorry for whichever teammate had tried to desperately save one or more lives, but failed. My heart ached for the one or more military families that would receive such dreadful news, like the family of that fallen soldier we honored at Kandahar Airfield.

As is required during wartime, my mind then shifted to my duties as an EOD officer. We were now down at least one man, which would put all of our lives at even greater risk during subsequent missions. I needed to call back home to our command, and then start working on a situation report. Next, I would need to—

"Brad, it's your father," my boss interrupted. "I just received this notification that your dad has … um … passed away."

He handed me a letter. To my utter disbelief, it was a notification from the Red Cross.

At my mother's request, I was being officially informed that my father, Michael William Snyder, was dead.

My dad?

I needed to call my mom. I had to not only find out how my father had died, but what I could do to help my mother and my siblings. As a dreadful combination of panic and grief began to set in during that terrible moment, it was so frustrating to be half a world away from the people I cared about most. Then, I felt completely helpless as I wondered what I was supposed to do.

"Let me know what you need, man," Fatty once again interrupted. "We're here for you … anything you need.

"I'm sorry," he said before slowly and quietly leaving the room.

While calling home and hearing my mother's anguish was extremely painful, I kept my emotions in check. I knew that somehow, I had to temporarily disconnect myself from my father's death. As officer in charge of a platoon of guys disarming bombs in Afghanistan, I had become accustomed to managing extraordinarily stressful situations in intense environments, especially while doing so almost every day. Tyler and Tara's respective deaths, coupled with the humiliation of my DUI arrest, had also gotten me used to operating out of a dark place. I was accustomed to the undertow of emotion at the back of my head, but had somehow become proficient at operating around it.

I resolved to go about the next few days as though my family tragedy was merely an administrative issue to resolve. As I spoke again to my mother, and subsequently to each of my siblings, I asked if they needed me to come home. After each said "no," it was surprisingly easy to tell them that I wasn't coming back. I had worked so hard to go on that deployment, and my job wasn't finished. I wasn't ready to come home and grieve.

I knew that I belonged in Afghanistan, and that my last few months there would be as close to a having a clear, defined purpose as I would ever get. For all I knew, I was about to be kicked out of the Navy because of my DUI. Instead of being welcomed home with a ticker-tape parade, I might have been well on my way to becoming a homeless veteran.

My platoon in Afghanistan needed me. It would have been difficult for my command to find a replacement with my experience and skill set, nor did I want them to try, especially after all the chaos I had caused with my stupid decision to drive drunk.

For a while, I sat down in my room and stared blankly. My thoughts wandered from issue to issue as I tried to work through what I should do in the wake of my dad's death.

I imagined my father in the room with me, sitting in a chair like the one I had just collapsed into. I could vividly imagine him sitting there wearing his boxy eyeglasses, worn-out golf shirt, and beat-up pair of shorts, much like the ones he used to mow the lawn in. I heard him tapping his wedding ring and the rack that held all my military gear, like he always did when he was giving me a lecture. This time, however, he wasn't saying anything,

"What should I do, Dad?" I asked.

He didn't answer. He just looked around the room as if he didn't hear me.

"Dad, what should I do?" I asked again.

This time, he acknowledged my question, looked at me, and shrugged his shoulders.

I started telling my father how hard I had worked to get where I was, and how I didn't want to give up what could be my last chance to work with such an extraordinary group of elite warriors. I probably wouldn't be allowed to do my job much longer, and besides, what was I going to do at home, anyway? Cry at my father's grave? I figured it would be better to grieve on my own terms.

Again, I asked my dad what to do.

My father simply sat across from me and shook his head in befuddlement. It was clear that my dad's ghost hadn't appeared to give me any help.

In that moment, I had a crazy feeling that's very hard to describe. Physically, it felt sort of like falling, but in my head, a different image came to mind. My room in Afghanistan faded, and suddenly, I was a child in front of my family's house in Florida; back on the street where I learned to ride my bike. In my imagination, I was learning to do so all over again.

At first, I struggled to pick up my bike, and struggled even more to hold it steady. I was definitely afraid of falling, but most of all, I was scared of failing. I wanted so badly to successfully ride my bike.

If I could, I would officially be a big kid, and most importantly, make my dad proud of me.

Suddenly, my father's ghost materialized behind me to give an assuring nod and smile before gripping the back of my bike's seat. He asked if I was ready, and even though I wasn't, I nodded anyway. My dad willed the bike forward as I felt his firm grip holding me upright. I began to pedal, faster and faster. At first I felt wobbly, but eventually, my hands and arms got the feel for the controls. I felt my dad's grip loosen, and I looked back. There he was, trotting next to me, urging me forward with words of encouragement.

"That's it, Brad," my father said. "You're riding a bike!"

I pedaled harder and began moving even faster than my dad could trot, but I had it now. Then, I gritted my teeth and pedaled as fast as I possibly could. I quickly turned my head and saw that my dad was still jogging, but slowly falling behind. After a while, I worried that he was gone, but when I had finally reached the end of the street, I realized that my father had been there all along.

His smile was beaming. As always, my dad had helped me succeed.

I didn't quite know how to work the brakes, and suddenly, I toppled over the handlebar. When I looked up from the ground, I was unhurt, but anxiously looking around. To my anguish, my dad was nowhere to be found.

Alone in my room in Afghanistan, I realized that from that moment forward, it was all up to me. I no longer needed to do things to make my father proud. I had to accomplish everything myself. I had always wanted to be my own man, and I had often butted heads against my dad's authority. That dynamic was now gone, and I was truly my own man.

Still, all I wanted was for my dad to give me advice or even scold me one more time. Or better yet, to congratulate me like after I dove into the water and conquered the monsters of Weeki Wachee Springs as a little boy, or when I set my personal best time in the swim meet that I didn't even win. Most of all, though, I just wanted to hear my dad say one more time that he was proud of me, and that he loved me.

The thought of truly being my own man was deeply unsettling, but I also knew that sitting around and moping wouldn't get me anywhere. If my dad's ghost had talked to me in that room, I knew he would have told me to move on and focus on my mission.

Even though my chain of command said that I could go home and be with my family during a time of grief, I decided to stay in Afghanistan. I told my superiors and teammates that I was fine, and that I wanted to press forward and finish out the deployment. My commanders were probably relieved that they wouldn't have to find a replacement, but at the same time, I knew they would keep a close eye on me.

I put the Red Cross' notification letter about my dad's death into a small desk drawer, and from that moment forward, acted as though I had never received it. In a strange way, I was able to set aside the fact that anything had happened and pick right up with our platoon's normal routine.

One night while watching a TV show called *Californication*, however, I encountered a scene where a father tells his son that despite some difficulties in their relationship, he was proud of him and loved him very much. The scene resonated so much that I absolutely lost it and began sobbing like a little girl. Thankfully, I was alone in my barracks room, which prevented the hardened warriors in my platoon from hearing me break down.

For a few minutes, I let it all out, as a year's worth—maybe even a few years' worth—of emotions poured from my eyes in seemingly endless streams of tears.

I don't recall exactly how long this lasted, but after calming down and clearing my eyes, I was able to keep my father's death in the drawer for the rest of my deployment to Afghanistan. I still had a job to do, and the best way to honor my father was to pour every ounce of myself into making sure that my brothers in arms made it home safely.

15

Somewhere Bright

On the morning of September 7, 2011, I sat atop the roof of a two-story mud-walled building, maintaining a security overwatch position for the rest of my platoon, which was gathered in the courtyard below me. For a moment, I was awestruck by the magnificent Afghanistan landscape and the beautiful sunrise.

Down in the courtyard, Fatty tinkered with radio equipment, trying with various levels of success to pass along updates to the battalion headquarters that was maintaining the command and control of our mission. Seated next to him, one of our interpreters had taken advantage of the lull in activity just around sunrise to catch a quick nap. As he snored gently, a walkie-talkie clipped to his body armor crackled to life. Voices began to chatter energetically in Dari, which is an Arabic dialect.

Fatty looked up from his radio equipment and punched the interpreter in the arm. The translator jerked awake and reflexively reached for his AK-47 before his sleepy confusion quickly wore off. His brow then furrowed as he focused on a conversation emitting from his walkie-talkie. A minute or two later, the translator urgently relayed that he was listening to two Taliban fighters trying to figure out the location of an American assault team.

The Taliban fighters spoke of two large helicopters that had dropped US soldiers off in the early morning. They didn't know, however, where the Americans were at the moment. Upon hearing this, a sly smile crept across the face of our SEAL commander. The enemy couldn't find us, but if they kept talking, he knew that we would soon find them.

After a few minutes, the TOC informed Fatty that they had been able to triangulate the location of the two Taliban fighters. He was also told that enemy forces were most likely gathering in a village about a kilometer to our northeast. In response, Fatty suggested that the assault team move in and engage. The mission was approved.

I gave my gear a once-over, then silently climbed down from the rooftop perch where I had watched over my teammates and witnessed that beautiful sunrise. In the courtyard below was the rest of the assault team, which was making last-second preparations to head out on patrol. My regular EOD partner, Evan, would be responsible for clearing an IED-free path and navigating the assault team, which would march like ants to the village where the enemy was believed to be gathering.

We had the element of surprise on our side, and still enough darkness to maintain an advantage over the gathering Taliban fighters. Still, an ambush or IED attack could obviously cause chaos at a moment's notice. We had to be ready.

Fatty twirled his finger in the air; the hand signal for "let's roll!" Evan then began clearing his way out of the compound before heading down the main path of the village leading north into the grape fields. Evan would subsequently zigzag us through a series of fields on our way to the next village, doing his best to keep us on a path free of IEDs, while also keeping us hidden and in the best possible fighting position in case we were attacked.

As always, progress was slow and difficult, but thankfully, we were able to make our way out of the first village. As I exited a group of mud-walled buildings, while about halfway back in the patrol, I saw a stack of fist-sized rocks arranged on my left, which looked like a pyramid at the center of a pathway. These rocks, which led to the west, gave me an uneasy feeling. Stacks like these were often used by locals to indicate pathways that were booby-trapped.

My gaze darted anxiously from the footsteps of the SEAL in front of me to the surrounding terrain, where I looked for any other tell-tale signs of potential IEDs. Perhaps I might find some freshly dug earth, a painted stone, or a colorful flag. Perhaps I might even see a few wires sticking out of the ground. I didn't, though, which led me to believe that my fears were probably misguided.

Aside from the hushed grunts and footsteps of assault team members, everything was quiet except for the chirping of birds and an occasional barking dog. If I hadn't been thinking about a Taliban ambush or an IED attack, it might as well have been a hike through the Sierra Nevada Mountains. If I make it out of Afghanistan, I thought, I will never take a quiet mountain hike for granted again.

Just then, a thunderous explosion jerked me out of my daydream, and a sickening blast wave ripped through the air. The pulverizing sound then echoed off the mountains and sent terrifying vibrations down my spine. When I looked up towards the front of our patrol, my stomach sank as I saw a black and gray mushroom cloud reach up into the air, which meant that someone had stepped on the hidden pressure plate of an IED. That person, I thought, was almost certainly my EOD partner, Evan.

For a terrifying thirty seconds, I listened to my radio hoping to hear Evan's voice. Thirty seconds felt like thirty minutes as nothing came across the radio. After also hearing nothing, Fatty, who had been near me in the patrol, looked back at me, and as our eyes met, we silently agreed that I would be needed up front. Where there was a blast, there were almost certainly casualties, along with potential secondary IEDs that could pose a serious threat to the rescue effort.

It would be my job to clear a safe area for a medic to tend to the wounded. I would then need to clear a landing zone for two UH-60 Black Hawk helicopters that would evacuate the casualties. The Taliban knew how vulnerable we were while caring for the wounded and would not hesitate to strike, so we would need to work quickly.

After running up to the front of the patrol, I encountered every EOD technician's worst nightmare. While I was simultaneously elated and confused to first see Evan and five SEALs huddling safely across a ravine to my left, I then saw an Afghan commando lying face down near a large crater. Both his legs had been blown off after stepping on a forty-pound IED.

The commando who had been standing behind him lay motionless on my side of the ravine. He had also sustained very serious wounds, as both his legs were gone. Both Afghans were unconscious, non-responsive, covered in blood, and had gruesome wounds exposed through their tattered uniforms.

A few other commandos were covered in dust from the explosion, with blood vessels in their eyes ruptured from the blast. I located an interpreter among them, who had also been very close to the blast. I grabbed him by his armor.

"Are you okay?" I yelled.

He weakly nodded. Even amid the carnage, I had no choice but to forcefully demand that he begin working with the remaining commandos to get them back in the game. We had to move these casualties right away, and I urgently needed their help.

As the interpreter began barking orders to the commandos in Pashto, some bravely nodded in acquiescence, while others shook their heads like cowards. They were simply too afraid to move their feet for fear of suffering a fate similar to their fallen brethren.

Evan yelled that he would work his way to the casualty on his side of the ravine, and asked me to work on evacuating the casualty nearest to the blast site. I agreed, and began doing what I could to clear a space around the downed commando. A SEAL named Leo followed me to help.

After a lot of hard work, Leo, a few commandos, and I were able to move the casualty—who was in bad shape but surprisingly not bleeding from any major arteries—to the back of the patrol. The medic took over from there, so it was time for me to go help evacuate the second casualty.

Moving the second wounded Afghan would probably be even more difficult, but thankfully, two members of the assault team were almost always carrying foldable stretchers on their backs. I shouted out for one, and in quick fashion, a commando from the back of the patrol came running up with a stretcher. As if we were running a relay, I grabbed the stretcher and began running toward the front of the patrol.

When I returned to the explosion site, I evaluated the terrain in front of me. To my left was the path Evan had chosen, which offered little footing and had a few trees blocking my way. The terrain to my right was mostly clear. I would have to cross the ravine on the other side of the blast hole before walking along another shorter wall on a patch of grass to reach Evan.

Thinking quickly, I preferred the clear path to my right, and the fact that I would be walking on grass was somewhat comforting, in that most IEDs are buried in exposed dirt. I leapt over the ravine, and began clearing towards Evan. That's when my entire world stopped.

Suddenly, I felt and heard a relatively gentle "pop." It was unlike any other blast I had ever witnessed. The explosion was not uncomfortable, and actually resulted in a sensation that felt like a click in my ears. It was almost like when your ears adjust to pressure when you're in an airplane.

Time stood still, as if I was in a tunnel. Then, I awoke in the fetal position on the grass. My vision was foggy, distorted, and mostly occluded. Even still, I was able to look down at my hands and determine that they were intact. I then looked down at my legs, and could make out the shape of my boots. I saw no blood, and while I couldn't be certain, I felt conscious. At the same time, I thought to myself that the "pop" must have been a blast, much like the one that tore apart two Afghan commandos just moments earlier. What in the world had just happened to me?

Considering the feeling of time standing still and an almost euphoric feeling of disconnection, as well as the fact that I couldn't see nor determine any injury, I became convinced that I had died. I had lost my life in a random field, in a country half a world from where I was born.

I looked at the blades of grass near my face—the only other objects that I could make out somewhat clearly—and tried to appreciate it as much as I could. I didn't know where I was headed next, but I figured that I should enjoy my last moments on earth as much as possible.

I began to think over my life. I thought about when I first started swimming, and how much I enjoyed growing up in the water, from Weeki Wachee Springs all the way to Annapolis. I thought about playing G.I. Joes with my brothers and "barber shop" with my sister.

I thought about leaving home for the first time. I thought about being a midshipman at the Naval Academy, where I shed my adolescence and finally learned how to lead.

I thought about my good friend Tyler, and how just maybe, I would get to see him again. Then, my thoughts drifted to Tara, who had decided to end her own life. Even in such an intensely confusing moment, the thought of possibly seeing her again scared me. Would she be the same on the other side, or would she be a tortured soul? Would she remember me? I feared the unknown, but the fact that I would be able to ask her why she chose to leave the world gave me respite. Perhaps I could finally be a source of protection and comfort for her in the afterlife. Maybe, in this new and different place, we could finally be together.

I thought of my dad and instantly rejoiced at the idea that we would soon be reunited. I became very excited about the prospect of filling him in on all of my adventures in Afghanistan, including the amazing platoon I served with and the brotherhood I had become a part of. I was certain he would be proud of me, and my heart swelled at the prospect of pleasing the father I had so recently lost.

I thought of my DUI, and worried for a moment that perhaps the other side wouldn't be a heaven, but a potential hell. Had I screwed up so badly that I might go to hell? Was there a hell? Would my service and ultimate sacrifice, along with the love for my brothers in arms and my country, be enough to compensate for my irresponsible mistake that endangered the lives of the passengers in the car that I hit?

I thought that if anyone knew the answers to these questions, it would be my Grandpa Lindsey. As a World War II veteran, my grandpa had been my first hero, and in many ways served as the person I hoped to become. Memories of my grandfather quickly flooded my consciousness, and I became convinced that he would be coming to take me wherever I was supposed to go. The fact that Grandpa Lindsey was coming convinced me that we were headed somewhere good, somewhere warm, somewhere bright.

As I accepted and reconciled my death, I became light, as though I was floating. The burden of my very existence had lifted, and I was happy and content to be moving on. Soon, I would learn the eternal secrets of the universe. Soon, I would be reunited with my departed family and friends. Soon, I would move on.

I thought of my mom, my brothers, my sister, and the others I would leave behind. My existential elation was temporarily curbed as I considered their heartbreak over my death. I wished that I could say, "I love you" just one more time. I wished that I could tell them what it felt like to die; how unexpectedly wonderful it is. I wished that I could tell them that I would wait for them on the other side. I would learn as much as I could before helping them across the pro-verbial finish line when it was their time. I didn't want them to be upset, but instead rejoice, as I was doing, over my transition.

I continued to lay on the ground in the fetal position, patiently waiting through split-second moments that seemed to stretch out for eternity. After a while, though, my euphoria started to wane, sort of like a fading sugar high. Doubt and fear then started to bubble at the bottom of my consciousness as I became uncertain over where I was and what had actually happened. What if I hadn't died?

The idea that I might still be alive began to blink in my head like neon lights. Just as that thought began to flicker, I became aware of an intense ringing in my right ear. Searing pain then began to shoot through my right hand and in flashes across my face. The ringing and shooting pain rapidly brought me back to reality, and in an in-stant, the elation and euphoria of dying was replaced with the fear and discomfort of living.

I became aware of significant damage to my face. I could hear blood dripping out of large lacerations, and it felt as though I no longer had lips. The fear amplified as I considered the damage and what it might mean. Would I be disfigured? Did I have a traumatic brain injury? Would I be a vegetable, forever trapped in my own body?

Over the ringing in my right ear, I heard Evan calling out to me. Warmed by the sound of my friend and knowing that I needed help, I called back to him, unable to hide the desperation and fear in my cries.

Following my voice through a thick cloud of dust and debris kicked up by the blast, Evan found me just outside another meter-wide blast hole. He grabbed me by my body armor and began assisting the medic in taking care of me. Aside from my bloody, shattered face, he and the medic didn't find any other significant wounds.

"How bad is it?" I asked Evan.

"Your face is pretty messed up, but the rest of you looks fine," he replied in a confident tone. "You're going to be okay, bud!"

His words echoed through my head: "You're going to be okay."

I'm going to be okay, I kept thinking. I'm going to be okay.

As the light continued to flicker, it became clear that I wasn't being led to the other side by my Grandpa Lindsey. I was being carried to a rescue helicopter by Evan and Leo.

As my brothers in arms hurried me toward the helicopter, I realized that I couldn't see what was in front of me. Before my very eyes, my life had changed forever.

16

In Between

I spent the next six days somewhere in between.

In reality, I was in Bethesda, Maryland. In my mind, I was in between Afghanistan and home; between consciousness and coma; between dreams and reality; between being alive and being dead. Pick any given point, and I wouldn't have been able to tell you precisely where I was. Location didn't seem to matter much, though, as the universe I perceived myself to be a part of didn't seem to subscribe to the usual rules.

Things like time and gravity now seemed to have no meaning, and this sensation caused an extremely unsettling feeling of disconnection. I was never quite sure if I was awake or asleep, and I was never quite sure what was real or a product of my imagination. To make matters worse, I didn't even realize that I was hallucinating for the first few days. The circumstances of my surroundings seemed to manifest, then fade away or morph just like in a dream sequence.

In one moment, I would be alone in a small green tent in the middle of a barren desert with its canvas walls flapping freely in the gentle warm breeze. This scene would then seamlessly transition to a beach, where I would be lying among kids and families playing volleyball and frolicking in the water. Then, I would be back in the desert, this time in a vehicle graveyard, with random car and motorcycle parts poking out of the desert floor in various stages of rust and decay.

I wandered the grand halls of museums before floating about above the earth in a seemingly endless forest of tall, evergreen trees. These surroundings morphed into each other so smoothly—with such vivid detail—that I had no reason to believe that I wasn't actually there. Soon, sounds from my reality actually began to populate in my dream world. I could hear the machines monitoring my vital signs, and without me realizing, these beeps and clicks would become birds or other things in my alternate reality.

I heard various commotions of nurses, therapists, doctors and surgeons all intent on repairing my real body. I was aware of this, but very distant. It wasn't that I didn't care; just that it was so far away from wherever I was that it was very difficult for me to focus on the sounds, or to glean any relevant information from them.

Instead, I wandered through the alternate realities without really being sure what to make of anything. Sometimes, I would become lucid enough to realize that something was wrong, and my dream sequences would take a turn. Pleasant beaches would become hellscapes, or I would get lost in the darkness, with no orientation as to up, down, left or right. Instead of grasping reality, it became easier to find my way back into my head and escape back to the beach. It was almost as if my mind had tripped over the inputs coming from the real world, and was not able to compute what was going on. My brain was functioning like a computer's screensaver.

I was aware that I was stuck, but I couldn't do anything about it. At times I was scared, but at other times, I would be at peace with being lost. It seemed like the deeper I fell into my own head, the more euphoric I became. Whenever I began to emerge, which caused my awareness of real life to increase, I would become frightened. Much like a turtle, I would then pull back into my dreamscape.

Amid the chaos of my alternate world, I heard a sound that pulled me back to reality. Echoing through the vastness of my mind was my mother's voice. I don't remember exactly what she was saying, but it was something simple like, "Brad … can you hear me? It's Mom."

She either repeated that a few times or it bounced around my head for a while. Either way, the warmth, nostalgia, and comfort of my mom's voice was the first thing that I could trust in this bizarre purgatory.

In an instant, I became aware that I had been in a dream world, but my mother's voice must be coming from reality. Suddenly, the world around me faded away, like the grains on an Etch A Sketch. I grabbed ahold of the sound like a life ring, and felt myself tugging up to the surface.

I woke up in a panic. There was no clock inside my alternate reality, but now I had the overwhelming feeling of a substantial amount of elapsed time. I hadn't really been present while wandering in the dreamscape, and instantly felt inundated with the burden of my body, which felt swollen, painful, and oddly encumbered.

I could feel my legs, but I could not move them. I tried to reach down with my right hand, but it was stuck on something. As I tugged, searing pain shot through my hand, causing me to grunt. I tried to sit up, but my whole body felt like lead, so I quickly gave up. I was glad to find that I could move my left hand, and I began feeling around, exploring my bed sheet and my hospital gown.

Before I got too far, my mother's slender hand grasped mine, and she began talking to me. At first, I didn't recognize her words, but her emotions were clear. She had been traumatized. She was trying to be strong, but I could feel the waves of sadness behind her words. She had been crying. She might have been crying right then. I grasped her hand in an attempt to comfort her. I wanted to hug her, but it was too difficult to move.

My head began to clear slightly, and I became aware for the first time that I could no longer see.

This thought registered, but with everything else going on, I didn't put much stock in it. I turned my head to ask my mother what happened, but as I tried to speak, all that came out was gargling. As I tried to use my mouth, tongue, and throat, I found that nothing worked. Then, as I moved my mouth, I became aware of a tube that seemed to run from my lips down into my throat. The tube prevented me from closing my mouth and using my tongue. Thus, I could make no sounds except for that subhuman gargle.

I found my inability to communicate unsettling, but as I became aware of the tube, I also became intensely uncomfortable at the thought of medical equipment being jammed down my throat. I began gesturing with my left hand, trying to call attention to the tube.

Two other voices emerged from the darkness. One voice I recognized to be my brother Russell's, while another belonged to an unrecognizable female.

My mother, brother, and the female voice all joined in an impromptu game of charades as I waved my left hand around wildly, obviously trying to communicate something. My frustration and anxiety mounted with every false guess as to what it was I was trying to say. I was desperately trying to call attention to the tube, hoping for an explanation or more importantly, for someone to remove the damn thing. As I became more and more excited, my gargles became louder and more pronounced, but unfortunately the hopeful guesses of family and a new friend seemed to address every detail but the tube.

"Do you want another pillow?" someone said.

"No!" I gargled.

"Do you want your bed elevated?" someone else asked.

"No!" I gargled again.

Finally, an idea occurred to me. I lifted up my left hand, pinched an imaginary pencil, and began making scribbling motions. My brother correctly guessed that I was asking for a pen and paper to write down my request. After a moment, I felt my brother's hands grasp mine, and he put a pen in between my fingers. He then pushed my hand down on a pad on the bed to my left. I began furiously scribbling "TUBE IN THROAT," to which my family began throwing out guesses that again missed the mark.

I was writing with my left hand (I'm right handed) while under the influence of heavy narcotic painkillers. Oh, and I couldn't see. My penmanship must have been terrible.

I tried again, working as hard as I could to exaggerate each letter of "T-U-B-E." Again, my family collectively sighed, unable to decipher my terrible writing. My frustration then bubbled over, and I lost my composure. I threw the pen across the room, and screamed every obscenity that popped into my head. Thankfully, they only came out in meager gargles, which probably would have been comical under different circumstances.

I listened to the hospital room's telemetry begin to beep frantically, reflecting my elevated heart rate as I panted and gargled out my frustration.

Then, I felt my brother come around to my left side, and put his hand on my shoulder.

"Brad, this is Russ," he said in a calm and loving voice. "I know this must be hard … but you just need to calm down."

Brotherly love is a funny thing, at least in the case of the relationship I have with my two brothers. We are all extremely close. This knowledge allows for a certain trust and honesty that is wonderful, but sometimes, honesty can be a funny thing.

Because I know my brother will always love me unconditionally, I can say things to him that I wouldn't dare to say to others. Russ and I confide in one another in a way that I can't imagine I would with anyone else, but I can also be hard on him in a way I wouldn't really be with anyone else. This is the true essence of unconditional love, and I am so thankful that I have that sort of a relationship with my brothers, my sister, and my mom. It was this unconditional love that gave me the freedom to express myself in that moment.

"Calm down?" I gargled while becoming enraged. "CALM DOWN?!

"F**K YOU!" I tried to say next, even more frustrated that my obscene words were coming out in gargling sounds.

At that moment, a clearer form of communicating finally came to mind. I balled my left hand into a fist and lifted my arm. I directed the back of my hand in the direction of my brother, and raised my middle finger.

As my middle finger stood in the center of my clenched fist, I wagged my hand back and forth slightly, for effect, pushing all of my anger and frustration into the gesture. Though I couldn't see it, I knew that Russ smiled, understanding my rage in a way that only a brother could.

In that moment, my brother probably knew that the tube, the broken bones, the stitches, the injury, the hospital room, and the rest were merely superficial conditions. The important thing was that I was alive, and right then and there, he knew that everything was going to be all right. As my swollen finger wagged in front of his face, he began to laugh, and he looked right at my mom.

"I think Brad is going to be fine!" Russ said.

His recognition of that moment, along with his laughter, had extinguished my anger. In a strange way, I felt comforted. Being there with my brother and my mom, I was able to anchor a part of my consciousness to the idea that I was alive, and that everything would eventually work itself out. Somehow, my brother knew that, and I did, too.

With my brother's hand on my shoulder and my now-relaxed left hand curled around my mother's hand, I became exhausted. I then drifted back to my alternate reality.

I wasn't able to tell the difference between minutes, hours, or days, but I bobbed up and down between reality and my dreamscape for what felt like a very long time. I managed not to tread as deep as I had before, and each time that I was able to poke my head above the surface into reality, I was able to aggregate more and more details about my situation.

Eventually, the dreaded tube was removed, and I was able to begin speaking in limited doses. A sort of rhythm emerged where I would bob up for a while, then either fall back into unconsciousness, or be put there in order to go into surgery. Moving back and forth was easier when it was voluntary. It was much harder to come back after the many individual operations.

During the third or fourth iteration of this rhythm, I wandered into a shipyard in my dreamscape. I had taken the details of my reality with me, and I was acutely aware of the fact that I was stuck inside my own head. I became convinced that the only solution was to find the way out of this shipyard.

I wandered about in a labyrinth of shipping containers stacked high in the air. With every corner I turned, there was another long corridor and another level of panic. Could I be stuck in my own head forever?

I wandered and wandered, becoming sure that I was only getting more lost. I began running to the end of each long corridor, only to find another, and then another. I tried to beat the system by climbing out of the maze, but I couldn't grip the sides of the containers or use my feet to leap.

My futile attempts at scrambling up the wall only added to my panic. Just as I had begun to contemplate giving up, a loud ripping sound echoed through the air. It was so loud that it seemed to make everything around me tremble and shake. I recognized it as the sound of Velcro. More specifically, it was the sound of the Velcro on a blood pressure cuff. I had heard this sound during prior hospital stays.

I realized that the sound was coming from reality, which I figured must be my ticket out of the never-ending shipyard. It was also, most likely, my ticket out of being permanently trapped in my own mind.

I closed my eyes and focused on the ripping noise. Again, I grabbed a hold of the sound as though it was a physical tether to the real world, and felt myself being lifted from the shipyard.

As I ascended, my dreamscape faded away, and was replaced by darkness. I returned to my real body, and felt a nurse removing the blood pressure cuff from my left arm. I began emphatically thanking her for taking my blood pressure, as it was the only way that I found my way back. I repeated that a few times, until I heard what I was saying and realized how crazy it sounded. Thankfully, the nurse just patted my shoulder and said, "You're welcome, dear!"

The nurse disappeared, and I sensed my mother approaching the bedside. She grasped my left hand in the comforting gesture I was growing accustomed to. My mother gently explained that because I was in an Intensive Care Unit (ICU), they were limiting the amount of visitors. My mom told me that a lot of people had stopped by to say hello, and that when I was willing and able, a lot of people would like to see me.

Most importantly, though, my sister Elyse was waiting outside. At the suggestion of bringing my sister into the room, I was instantly horrified, and began formulating a protest.

I am eight years older than my sister, and we are very close. I cherish our relationship, and have always tried to be a good older brother. I love her deeply, and have always wanted Elyse to know that no matter what, I would always be there to love and support her.

I have also tried to be a positive role model, and I like to think I am a bit of a "hero" to her. To be honest, I am not big into the word "hero," especially when it's in reference to me, but in the case of my sister, I'm okay with it.

When my mom said that Elyse wanted to see me, I was terrified for two primary reasons, one more selfish than the other. For one, I have always embraced the idea that my sister lived in a somewhat naive version of the world, sort of like looking through Disney-colored glasses. I liked the idea that she and her girlfriends spent most of their time talking about new bands and cute boys, and I was comforted that she was somewhat sheltered from the evil that had become my job to fight. I now know that this is a bit ridiculous, but it's the way I viewed things at the time.

I didn't want my baby sister to see me because my face now reflected all the ugliness of the world that I had tried to shelter her from. I had gathered enough details to know that my face and body were grotesquely swollen. I had large burn marks up my right arm and across some of my chest. My eyes were swollen shut and hidden amongst a maze of long, hideous lacerations across my face. Some of the wounds were pulled together with stitches of black thread, while others were too wide and were instead packed with gauze. My head was shaved, and my skin reflected every color except a natural flesh tone. I probably looked much more like Frankenstein's monster than any version of Brad that Elyse might recognize.

I was frightened by how she might react and what my image might represent in her mind about the picture-perfect world she had lived in until that point. I had tried so hard to shelter Elyse, but now, I would be the one to deliver the bad news about the real world. There is indeed another side that the Disney Channel doesn't show you.

The other reason I didn't want Elyse to see me—the more selfish reason—goes back to that "hero" image that I hoped she would maintain. To her, I was a badass. I wore a pristine white uniform, decorated in colorful medals reflecting all the cool things I had done. She saw me as a guy who could do amazing stuff like jump out of planes, SCUBA dive, and take apart bombs. I liked the idea that maybe she bragged about me to her friends. I liked the idea that in her mind, I was what I had always hoped to be. I liked the idea that she was proud of me.

I didn't want Elyse to see this broken version of her big brother. I didn't want her to see the guy who had gotten drunk and crashed his car into another, and wound up in jail. I didn't want her to see the guy who failed at his job, missed an IED, and got blown up. I didn't want her to see my ugly face. I wanted to live on in her mind as that perfect and pristine "Hero Brad." In some ways, "Old Brad" only existed in her mind, and if she saw me this way—broken and ugly—Hero Brad would be gone forever.

Before I could voice my protest, I felt my mom's hand slip away, only to be replaced with the hand of my sister.

"Hi, Brad," was all that Elyse said at first.

It took all I had not to let my swollen, heavily bandaged eyes overflow with tears. Here I was before her, a representation of all the terrible things in the world. Not a hero, but a truly broken man. I felt as though I had failed her. I felt as though I was a disappointment. I felt as though I had let her down.

Shattered and humbled, I said what I always had to my little sister since she was a baby: "Hello, sweetheart."

I braced for what I expected to be an emotional reaction, during which Elyse would voice her disappointment in me. But that's not what happened. Instead, she said that she loved me, and leaned in to give me a hug.

I had sold my sister short. She wasn't disappointed. She didn't live in a Disney Channel version of the world; she lived in the real one, just like me. Try as I might to shelter Elyse from evil and ugliness, she already knew it existed. She didn't care about Hero Brad, nor did she see me as Ugly Brad. She just saw me as Brad, and loved me for being her older brother. She knew I wasn't perfect; she was just glad to have me back.

I don't know if my broken face reflected it, but I know for sure that I sobbed on the inside. In that moment, I realized that Old Brad was dead and gone. There was no longer any existence or validity to the notion of Hero Brad. My old uniform and its colorful medals were just that: A uniform with medals. They were not me.

On the flip side, I was not broken and ugly. I was not a function of my mistakes. I was just me. I didn't have to live with the burdens of my past any longer. In that moment, my sister gave me the best gift anyone could ever give: she gave me freedom from myself. By shedding my self-image and my expectations, I was now free to rebuild myself and to transform. As enlightening as that moment was, the drugs were still pumping through my veins in relatively high volumes, and before long, I succumbed to sleep and my strange dreamscape.

Though I was in and out of surgery nearly every day, I managed to spend more time in reality and less in between. I still hallucinated, but also found ways to manage it. From time to time I would slip, and ask my mother or sister about a strange bunny at the end of my bed (of course, there was no bunny at the end of my bed).

We got through each day by breaking it down into a series of individual moments. Each hour, there would be some sort of activity or goal that needed to be accomplished, and by the end of each day, we managed to see some sort of progress in various forms. I was awake longer, speaking more clearly, on less and less painkillers, and more mobile.

The elephant in the room (figuratively speaking; I wasn't hallucinating an elephant) was the extent of my vision loss. It had been acknowledged that there was severe damage to both eyes, but I felt like everyone, including me, had refused to put any stock in any concept other than my vision eventually returning. From my perspective, I just kept thinking that there was a bandage over my eyes, and eventually they would heal. The swelling would subside, the bandage would be removed, and I would be able to see again. There was no doubt in my mind, in fact, that this was the case.

My true concerns were vain in that I was most worried about how I was going to look after everything healed. I knew that I had suffered very serious wounds to my face, and wondered how lasting the damage would be. Were my facial features permanently crooked and askew? Would the scars last as ugly red caterpillars stretching across my face?

On my sixth day in Bethesda, four surgeons entered our small hospital room to explain what had happened in Afghanistan, and how they were trying to repair me.

As the doctors outlined my injuries, I realized that the head of my metal detector must have just missed the IED buried in the grass between me and the injured Afghan commando. As I charged to his aid, my foot landed on a license plate-sized pressure switch. It consisted of two pieces of scrap metal separated by small pieces of foam, likely salvaged from a junkyard chair or a derelict motorcycle.

As my body weight overcame the small bits of foam, the metal contacts connected to an electronic circuit. When the switch closed, nine volts of stored energy were released from an alkaline battery, just like the one you might find in your smoke alarm. The current created by this release flowed through a short length of wire and into a blasting cap nestled among forty pounds of ammonium nitrate fertilizer explosive, which was contained by a thick plastic double-wide milk jug. The current passed through a small filament inside the blasting cap, which heated up and ignited a tiny primary charge within the cap. This relatively small detonation ignited the ammonium nitrate.

In fractions of a second, the rapidly combusting explosive emitted a powerful blast wave that rippled out through the ground and then into the surrounding area. At first, the wave hit my face, ripping through the flesh of my cheeks and down my chin. The wave then pushed my protective sunglasses up my forehead, which left behind an ugly open wound tracing its path. My right eye was filleted open and fully exposed.

The blast wave then slammed into my chest, pushing my rifle so hard against my chest plate that the weapon's barrel actually bent around my body, ensuring that I would never fire it again. As the blast wave then pounded through the rest of my body, it felt like going a few rounds with Mike Tyson.

The blast wave finally lost its power as it continued outward, but it was immediately followed by a massive amount of primary and secondary fragmentation cast outward by the exploding fertilizer. A menacing plume of melted pieces of plastic milk jug, dirt, and rocks erupted from the ground, following the path of destruction left by the preceding blast wave.

My face, neck, arm, and body was barraged by the shrapnel, which opened up wounds wherever contact was made with my skin. While my left eye had survived the initial blast wave unharmed, it didn't fare as well against the onslaught of fragments: a small rock penetrated the orbit of my left eye. Due to my proximity to the IED, the lower half of my body was thankfully spared from the brunt of the damage. My face, however, took the worst of it.

In front of my mother, brother, sister, aunt, and uncle, the surgeons announced that there would be one last major surgery before I would begin (more or less) a full-time recovery process. The wounds on my face had been healing, and would now be left alone, for the most part. The facial lacerations had been healing so well, in fact, that my sister had said that I reminded her of Wolverine from *X-Men*, who had a supernatural ability to quickly heal his wounds.

The four surgeons explained that the upcoming surgery would address the issues afflicting both of my eyes. Unfortunately, the doctors admitted, the damage to my left eye was too severe to salvage, and the risk of infection was so high that they needed to remove the eye entirely.

I found this news devastating, as my mental image of a guy with only one eye looked extremely freakish. My initial reaction was sadness over the perception that I would forever appear to be abnormal and ugly.

The doctors went on to reassure me that this would not the case. They explained how they would implant a small prosthetic mount that would be stitched to my eye muscles. This would allow me to retain eye movement, even though I wouldn't be able to see on my left side.

While the damage had been extensive on the right side, the physicians believed there was a chance that they could salvage my damaged retina and re-adhere it to the back of my eye, with hopes of some of my vision returning.

"How much of my vision might come back?" I asked the doctors.

"Lieutenant Snyder," the surgeon replied. "You will have a less than one percent chance of being able to perceive light and dark with your right eye."

In that moment, I knew that I would be blind for the rest of my life.

As that stark reality struck me for the first time, I hung my head, and admittedly indulged in a moment of self-pity. At the same time, I was aware that every eye in that room—every eye that worked, anyway—was fixed squarely on me. Everyone was assessing how I would react to this devastating news.

I used my mind's eye to visualize the room. I saw my family members gathered around. They were all there to love and support me. When I visualized my brother, I was reminded of what unconditional love meant. When I visualized my sister, I was reminded that she would love me regardless of how I looked or what I was capable of. She loved me as Brad—her older brother—nothing more, nothing less.

I thought of how I got here. It was me who signed on that dotted line and put myself in harm's way, on purpose. I was aware of the risks when I joined the Navy. I was further reminded of those risks when Tyler had been killed in Iraq. I had taken responsibility for my future, and decided that no matter what the level of sacrifice, my service was worth it.

Why should that change now? How could I be a victim in this situation? There was no one to blame but myself.

I thought back to that moment on the battlefield where I saw my grandfather and thought that I was dead. I wasn't. I was very much alive, and surrounded by people who loved me unconditionally. So what if I couldn't see them? It didn't mean that they weren't there.

I thought of Tyler, and how he didn't get to come back alive from war, while I did. Right then, I decided to take responsibility for my future. I decided to appreciate the encouragement that my family had been showing me all along, and learn to live with what I had, instead of dwelling over what I no longer had.

Blindness would be a daunting challenge. I had faced tough challenges before, though, and found some measure of success. This would be no different.

Being blind wouldn't define nor confine me. Armed with the love of my family, I would continue to grow, develop, learn, and pursue happiness with the same vigor as before I was injured. The only difference was that this time, I would have to try to conquer a world that I couldn't see.

The surgeons left the room, and once again, I slipped away. When I awoke, the room was quiet and still. I was alone except for my mother and the nurse, who leapt up to go inform the surgeon that I was awake.

Moments later, the surgeon came in to discuss the surgery on my eyes that he and his fellow physicians had just performed. Indeed, they hadn't been able to save the retina of my right eye. What they thought was my retina had actually been an enlarged blood vessel.

It turned out that I had lost the retina completely in the blast. The doctor said that he was sorry, and excused himself from the room.

I heard my mom begin to cry. I reached out next to me for her hand in an effort to provide comfort. To my own surprise, I wasn't sad upon hearing the news. Somehow, I had expected it.

My resolution was firm. Blindness would not become an obstacle. I knew that just as I knew that the sky was blue, even though I could no longer see it.

With my weeping mother at my bedside, I told her not to worry. "We're going to be okay," I whispered.

17

Tap, Advance

Using a five-foot-long white cane with a red tip, I tapped the linoleum tile floor of the hospital's long hallway a pace ahead of my left foot. Content that the area was clear of any obstacles, I stepped forward. I then tapped the floor a pace ahead of my right foot. Again finding nothing, I advanced.

The alternate tapping sound made by my cane striking the tile echoed through my brain, which was still foggy due to the latent effects of painkillers. Thankfully, those drugs were now being administered in minimal doses.

I no longer needed an IV, which had allowed me to get up and start moving. At first, it had been a struggle to find my way to the toilet, and even more of a struggle to find my aim. But before too long, I had become comfortable making my way back and forth. This effort had been exhausting initially, but day-by-day, I became stronger and stronger. Each day, I woke up ready to tackle a new challenge.

Tap, advance. Tap, advance. Tap, advance. That's how my rehabilitation process went. One challenge fed into another.

As I slowly made my way down the long corridor, the voice of the therapist guiding me through this painstaking process echoed through my head.

"You don't have to bow your head and shrug your shoulders like that . . . what are you afraid of?" she said. "Trust your cane!"

What am I afraid of?

"Everything . . . " I muttered.

In addition to a drug-induced fog in my brain, my hearing was substantially impaired due to a right eardrum rupture that I suffered in the blast. This, coupled with the idea that I was envisioning my environment audibly for the first time, made for a very scary rendering in my mind.

The long hospital corridor seemed more like an endless black cavern filled with all sorts of scary monsters, much like when I dove into Weeki Wachee Springs as a boy. More than two decades later, these monsters all seemed ready to leap out and strike when I least expected it. Subconsciously, I had been bracing for this inevitable attack, but the therapist was right. Just because I couldn't see the world didn't mean that it had all of a sudden transformed into a scene from *Alien vs. Predator*. The world was just as it had been before, and I needed to trust in these new techniques in order to find my way through it.

I stopped for a moment, took a deep breath, relaxed my shoulders, and lifted my head. I made a deliberate effort to put aside the thought of demons in the darkness, and to move forward with confidence.

Tap, advance. Tap, advance. Tap, advance.

At the end of the long hallway, my therapist instructed me to turn left, and we worked our way down another long hallway. As we came upon a set of elevators, my cane struck the metal doors with a loud "TWANG!" We took the elevator down to the first floor, slowly walked down two more hallways (as my therapist offered guidance and encouragement along the way), and then finally, into a large room that I recognized to be a gym. It had that rubbery, sweaty odor, along with the faint stench of bleach.

Instead of folding up a metal detector, I now had to fold up a cane. After I did so, I was ushered to a treadmill by the therapist. I grabbed hold of the handrails on both sides and set my feet on the large rubber tread. The therapist put one hand on my hip to ensure I was steady, and pushed a button to start the tread below my feet.

I began walking to keep up with the treadmill's slow roll. Initially, I was dismayed by how fast my heart rate elevated during such a minimal amount of exertion, but at the same time, I was just glad to be up and moving. Twenty minutes later, the treadmill's roll came to a halt, which prompted me to climb down.

"How far did I go?" I asked while huffing and puffing.

"Just under one mile," the therapist replied enthusiastically as she handed me my cane.

One year earlier, I could hike a mile in my sleep, like that day in Afghanistan when my platoon found out we had to walk back to base after forty-eight hours of hiking through the desert. It was strange to be proud of a physical accomplishment that used to mean so little, but considering what had happened to me, walking nearly a mile felt pretty damn good.

Tap, advance. Tap, advance. Tap, advance.

The next day, I was able to go a mile and a half in the same amount of time. Later in the week, I was able to start jogging, even though I always had to keep a careful, firm grasp on the handrails.

By this point, I had been in Maryland for just under three weeks, and the hospital's staff agreed that my condition had improved to a point where I could be transferred to a VA facility near my mother's home in St. Petersburg. There, I could continue my recovery and rehabilitation.

Tap, advance.

I LOOKED DOWN AND saw my hand gripping the black rubber handle of my long, white cane. This time, the red tip of the cane sunk into fine white sand. I looked up, and quickly realized that I was on a beautiful beach, one that I remembered well. It was on Anna Maria Island on Florida's Gulf Coast, where we used to go for pancakes every Sunday morning when I was a kid.

I saw the long, green pine needles of tall trees wave in the gentle breeze. The roots of the trees disappeared into the fine white sand, which led to the giant blue ocean. Where the ocean ended, the sky began with its light blue color adorned by streaks of wispy white clouds.

Just ahead of me, I saw my family laying out towels, setting up a spot for a long day at the beach. I watched for a moment as they chatted excitedly with one another, undoubtedly developing a strategy for the rest of the day. We would do some boogie boarding, followed by some sandcastle construction and a brief lunch break before heading back into the surf. I don't know why we would always discuss our plan, because that's what we did every time our family visited the beach.

My mother looked up and was the first to notice me. She then began to wave and beckoned me to join them, which prompted me to start making my way towards her.

As I tapped the sand in front of me, it occurred to me that it was silly for me to do so. Why did I have this cane anyway? Wait … wasn't I blind? Isn't that why I have the cane? Well, if I'm blind, then this isn't so bad. I can see just fine. What do I even need this cane for?

Just as I tossed away my cane and began to jog towards my family, the dream faded, and was replaced with pitch black. I wasn't on Anna Maria Island. I was in the VA Hospital in Tampa, Florida.

For the first time since the blast, I woke up in the hospital alone. Right then and there, it fully dawned on me that I was blind, and that I would be this way for the rest of my life.

As if that epiphany wasn't painful enough, I realized that every night, I was going to dream dreams where I could see just fine. Then, every morning, I would wake up to darkness. Every single day for the rest of my life, I knew that I would be reminded—in the cruelest way possible—that I was blind.

All of a sudden, my positive perspective faded. Despite a "can do" attitude, the weight of this new, permanent darkness seemed to encircle me and pull downward. I began to feel claustrophobic: forever confined by the darkness around me.

I reached to the nightstand and found the talking iPhone that I had been given only a few days earlier. After fidgeting around, I voice-dialed the only number that I knew off the top of my head: my mom's. I told her what had just happened, and said that I didn't know if I could handle waking up every morning to beautiful dreams replaced by endless darkness, which served as such a harsh reminder of my blindness.

My mom thought about what I said for a moment, then replied.

"Brad, you're looking at it all wrong," she said. "You just have to flip your perspective.

"Instead of dreading every morning when you're reminded that you're blind, you just have to look forward to the end of each day," my mom continued. "That's when you'll get your vision back, if only for a while."

Her remarks made a strong impact. I suppose it was a reminder of things I already knew, but in such an emotional moment, my mother's reassurance was exactly what I needed.

She was right. I didn't want anyone to attend my pity party, and I knew that I didn't want to be there, either. Feeling sorry for myself wouldn't lead anywhere good. The sooner I accepted my situation, the sooner I could find a way to move forward, and the happier I would be.

From that day forward, I didn't waste any time looking backward, where all I could see was darkness. I only concerned myself with the present, and how to move into the future. At least I could see in my dreams.

Tap, advance. Tap, advance. Tap, advance.

I HEARD THE TAP of a cane just like mine strike the metal doorframe of my hospital room. Only this time, it wasn't my cane, which was folded on the bedside table.

The cane in the doorway belonged to US Army Captain Ivan Castro, who had been blinded in 2006 when a mortar landed near his position in Iraq.

As he stepped inside my room, I could hear the jingle of the heavy amount of flair worn by most soldiers. This sound, coupled with the click of finely polished Oxford shoes, made it easy for me to imagine Captain Castro dressed sharply in his Army uniform.

Ivan introduced himself and told me that his hand was outstretched. It took me a moment to find it, but we finally shook hands, which made me smile at the inherent humor in two blind guys waving their hands around trying to find each other.

I clumsily directed the wounded combat veteran to a chair next to my hospital bed, and he took a seat. Ivan began telling me the story of his injury, how he learned of his blindness, and how he adapted. I found it humbling to learn that Ivan's injuries had been much more extensive than mine, but yet, here he sat. Captain Castro was still on active duty in the Army, and was speaking almost nonchalantly about an experience that had so dramatically changed his life.

Ivan admitted that there had been tough moments along the way, including surgical setbacks, failed relationships, and bouts with depression over a life in the dark. Still, he had managed to find his way through it. I asked him how.

"One step at a time, just like everyone else," Captain Castro said. "Don't be a victim … that won't get you anywhere."

Simply put, but so incredibly potent.

Ivan told me that his first goal had been to run in the Army's "ten-miler" race in Washington, and then the Marine Corps Marathon. One challenge had led to another for Ivan, and he was progressing brilliantly.

I was so impressed by Ivan. He was not defined by his blindness; he was the same person he had been all along: strong, capable, self-motivated, and self-aware. He was a warrior who wasn't going to let anything slow him down. Ivan was the first blind person I had ever met, and he had successfully managed to forge a new life in the dark.

I had so many questions for Ivan. What was it like to be blind in everyday life? Did he get used to it? Did the dreams go away or change? Did people look at him funny or treat him differently? What was it like to go on an actual "blind date?"

Ivan answered all of my questions candidly, relaying experiences of traveling all over the country in hectic airports, how he had met his new wife, and how they had just welcomed a new baby girl. I listened in awe, not able to even consider working my way through a busy airport, let alone changing a baby's diaper.

Yet, here sat Ivan. Only six years prior, he had been right where I was: lying in a hospital room, confused and afraid. Now, he had a career, a wife, and a baby daughter. By taking everything one challenge at a time, he had seemingly figured it out.

Even though neither of us could see, Ivan showed me what a blind guy looked like. He showed me that I wasn't alone in the dark. He showed me that it was possible to be the same person that I was. He showed me that it would be challenging, but that I could live my life just as I would've before my injury. He showed me that eventually, you can not only get used to the darkness, but thrive in it.

Tap, advance. Tap, advance. Tap, advance.

TO HELP PAINT A mental picture of my surroundings, my family instituted a "celebrity look-alike" game. Every new person I met along the way would be evaluated by my mother and siblings, and assigned a celebrity look-alike, which meant that my nurses in Walter Reed had included Cameron Diaz, Reese Witherspoon, and Shania Twain. My brother Mitch had a particular aptitude for this game, and rapidly became the authority on celebrity look-alikes.

The next person through my hospital room door at the Tampa VA was my new physical therapist—a bubbly young blonde, I was told—named Lindsay. Her celebrity look-alike was Jessica Alba, which served as extra motivation to succeed. Lindsay picked up right where I had left off with my previous physical therapist in Maryland. Before we even had a chance to dive into small talk, she had me up on a treadmill, and this time, I was running.

After a few days, Lindsay suggested that we up the ante and try running outside. Up until that point, I had spent minimal, if any, time outside, so I leapt at the opportunity to get some fresh air. Lindsay enlisted the help a fellow physical therapist, Jenny, a slender brunette who I was told looked just like Demi Moore. While the concept of "guide-running" made me a little uneasy at first, picturing Jessica Alba and Demi Moore shielding me from other runners and obstacles helped paint a pleasant mental picture.

Lindsay guided me outside to an asphalt pathway that looped around the VA facility. I held just above her left elbow, and we were off. It was tricky at first as I learned to adjust to Lindsay's movements, but quickly, the two of us were able to establish trust. Before too long, guide-running felt totally natural, as if this was how I had been doing it all along. At points along the run, I was actually able to push the pace of the girls, just above where they were comfortable.

After two laps around the mile-long loop, we stopped to catch our breath and grab a sip of water. Excited and energized by our rapid progress, Lindsay suggested that we try a local 5k race, just for fun. Sharing her enthusiasm, Jenny and I agreed.

Tap, advance. Tap, advance. Tap, advance.

When I was young, I had trained almost every day at the Northshore Aquatic Center on the west side of Tampa Bay. Just to the swimming facility's south is the historic Vinoy Resort and aptly named Vinoy Park, also along the water. If you followed the coastline south, you would run into the St. Petersburg pier: a quarter-mile-long protrusion into Tampa Bay with a strange upside down pyramid structure at the end, where you could find a few restaurants and shops.

The end of the pier would mark the starting line for the Creaky Bones 5k, which was always scheduled for the Thursday before Halloween. The day of the race would also mark one week before the hospital would officially give me clearance to leave the facility.

Lindsay had pulled a few strings, and the staff agreed to look the other way while she, Jenny, my mom, and I packed into a van and drove around Tampa Bay to the race. Wrapped up in the excitement, my mom had agreed to run the race with us. If you knew my mom, you would know what a big deal this was. At the time, my mother hadn't run at all since playing youth softball about forty years earlier. Admitting that she wouldn't be able to run much of the race, my mom had resolved to at least walk the full distance, which meant a great deal to me.

The pier was a festive commotion. As we wandered about in search of the registration table, Jenny and Lindsay took turns describing the variety of crazy costumes sported by other runners. Among the ghosts and ghouls, we found the right table, and finally, the starting line.

The fog in my brain had finally cleared a few days earlier, but it seemed to return as we stood in the excited crowd. It became very difficult for me to filter out all the sounds that differed amid the chaos, and it truly felt as though I was in the dark, both literally and figuratively.

Lindsay must have sensed my elevated stress level, because she started giving me a hilarious description of a fellow runner's hideous spandex outfit. Her words not only relaxed me, but prompted me to clasp her elbow and hold tightly. In that moment, I fully placed my trust in Lindsay to guide me through the noisy darkness.

Out of nowhere, the starting gun went off, which scared the living daylights out of me. For a fraction of a second, I was back in Afghanistan, trying to figure out where the shots were coming from. I flashed back to the Afghan soldier and me unleashing gunfire toward the insurgents who had fired mortars in our direction. My heart started to pound as if I was right back in the middle of that field of fire.

Suddenly, I was jerked back to the St. Petersburg pier when Lindsay took off running, which helped both of us avoid being trampled by the large crowd of runners behind us. Despite her best efforts, what had been loud and chaotic before had only gotten worse. I was now lost amid the steady beating footsteps of hundreds of fellow runners.

While searching around my audible senses, I found not only the sound of my beating heart, but my own two feet pounding on the asphalt. Immediately, I focused entirely on that sound and ignored everything else. Once I got used to it, I would be able to find the sound of Lindsay's feet, and then Jenny's.

As we left the pier, the terrain turned from asphalt, to brick, to cement, back to asphalt, then up a curb, and finally, onto a sidewalk.

Before each change, Lindsay would describe what was coming, and I would ensure that my feet were ready. Jenny also chimed in with descriptions of our surroundings or nearby runners.

As the race progressed, the crowd began to thin out, which made it much easier to perceive the world around us. I settled into our pace and began to find comfort in the exertion. We passed the resort on our left, and then the park on our right. As we approached the pool I used to train in, I heard the familiar sounds of a swim meet: the starting buzzer and the splashes of young swimmers, along with the corresponding cheers from their families and teammates. It sent a chill down my spine to consider that only a decade earlier, I had been one of those young swimmers competing on a similar Florida fall evening.

Here I was, after going around the world, dying, and somehow coming back. The feeling was a bit scary, but also as comforting as the warm air I felt on my face while running. For the first time in a long time, I felt things coming full circle.

When we reached the halfway point of the race, I asked Lindsay how many people were behind us. I didn't care if I was blind; I was still a competitor.

"Don't worry," Lindsay said between breaths. "There are lots!"

I smiled, and this time, urged her forward by lightly pressing Lindsay's elbow. The sidewalk turned to cement, then to bricks, and then back to asphalt. After a few minutes of intense exertion, Lindsay, Jenny, and I sprinted through the finish line surrounded by a cheering crowd.

Elated, we swapped hugs, but the moment was fleeting as soon as we remembered that my mom was still out on the course. We turned around and jogged a quarter-mile back to the end of the pier, where we would wait for her to arrive.

After a few, brief moments, Lindsay saw my mom walking briskly toward the finish line. We jogged over to her, and without saying a word, Lindsay took my hand and put it on my mother's elbow instead of hers.

"Let's finish together, Mom!" I said.

I couldn't see her, but I'm sure my mom was nodding emphatically, perhaps with a tear in her eye. While running the longest distance she had in forty years, my mother guided me through the last quarter-mile of the 2011 Creaky Bones 5k.

Tap, advance. Tap, advance. Tap, advance.

THE FIRST FRIDAY OF that November also marked the first time that the VA officially granted me permission to leave the hospital over a weekend. I would be allowed to relax at home from Friday evening until Sunday evening, at which point I would be required to return to undergo the following week's therapies and treatments.

My face was still healing from the blast and a bone in my right hand was still broken, but otherwise, my health was rapidly returning. As the injuries faded, my focus on adapting to blindness was stronger than ever. But before doing anything else, it was time to celebrate First Friday.

First Friday had always been a monthly celebration of sorts in downtown St. Petersburg, not far from the pier. An entire block of bars and restaurants was closed off to traffic, and beer vendors would set up shop on all corners while bands played live music. In 2011, the party just so happened to coincide with my breakout from the hospital. In addition, my friends in the area had arranged for a portion of all First Friday proceeds to benefit my family, as well as the families of other wounded service members undergoing lengthy periods of rehabilitation. Of course, I was very touched by this gesture, and wanted to attend the party to personally thank my friends for all of their incredible support.

My friend Rick, with whom I had served in Virginia Beach, had flown in with his girlfriend to visit for the weekend. Along with my brother Mitch, we piled into a car and made our way downtown. Just like I had experienced on the pier, the loud music and the sounds of people celebrating initially overwhelmed me. Once again, I found myself feeling alone in the darkness, and this time, I didn't have a trained professional like Lindsay or Jenny to rely on.

Still, Mitch and Rick managed to keep me calm by cracking jokes and always staying close. Someone jammed a beer into my hand when we arrived at the party, but after only one sip, I found myself slipping back into the fog that I had just managed to get out of my brain. I passed the beer along to my brother, who graciously accepted it.

Rick and Mitch maneuvered our group into a quieter area, and soon, a crowd of my old friends gathered around us. I was flattered by the turnout, and glad to catch up with so many people who meant so much to me. After a little while, though, I became dismayed by how many of them said that they were sorry, and how they had been so sad to hear the news of my injury.

I wasn't sure how people were supposed to react to such news, but I didn't like that I had made so many people upset. For years, I had been the guy who usually made people laugh and smile, and I didn't like the idea that I had brought anyone down.

I was also used to being a very capable person: jumping out of planes, diving into the depths of the ocean, and taking apart bombs. I was the guy who went into harm's way so other people didn't have to. I didn't want anyone to worry about me, and I certainly wasn't seeking out any pity.

"I'm just fine now! Things like this happen," I would say to my friends, along with, "Don't worry about me … I feel great!" Another line I used was, "You should have seen me a few weeks ago."

Despite my repeated attempts to lighten the mood, friends kept coming over to hug me and cry, and to say how upset they had been upon hearing about my injuries. Make no mistake: I appreciated their sentiments. But after a few more minutes, I felt like shouting at the top of my lungs.

"DON'T WORRY ABOUT ME!" I wanted to yell. "I'M FINE!"

I didn't, of course, and if I had been one of my friends, I suppose I would have said all the same things that night. Still, I needed a way to show everyone that I was fine. I needed a way to show everyone that I was going to be okay. I needed a way to show everyone that nothing had changed. I was the same as I had always been; I just couldn't see now. The fact that I was blind wasn't going to change my hopes of a happy, successful life. As the party continued, I wanted so badly to find a way to show everyone how I felt inside.

Just then, I heard a familiar gruff voice.

"Hey Brad, how are ya feeling?" the man said.

I subsequently recognized the voice as my former swim coach, Fred Lewis. Fred was an old-school tough guy who didn't put up with any nonsense, especially as a coach. The unforgettable Mickey Goldmill character from *Rocky* is probably the best comparison.

Ever since Fred became my coach when I was fifteen, he didn't waste one second on trying to become friends. His job was to push me hard, and when I improved, to push me even harder. Fred never let up on me, and in doing so, he helped turned me into a man, and eventually, a warrior.

Because I owed so much to Fred, encountering him at the First Friday party left me initially speechless. For a moment, I worried that he might be disappointed in me. Did he know that stepping on the IED in Afghanistan had been my fault? Would he be saddened or hurt by the news of my injury? Had I let him down?

For a moment, I heard Fred's voice crack. He wasn't disappointed, but like the others, he had been deeply affected by the news. At the same time, the crack in his voice indicated that he was happy to see me, and even happier that I was alive. To my amazement, this tough old man was proud of me.

Before he could say anything else, I reached out and gave him a quick hug, which I never could have imagined doing just a few years earlier. Once we broke our brief embrace, Fred returned to his typical no-nonsense demeanor.

"When are you coming back to practice?" he said.

Fred knew me, and he knew that I didn't want to be pitied. He knew that I had become a warrior, and I just needed a challenge to jumpstart the rest of my life. Fred always knew exactly how to push me forward, which was what made him such a great coach and wonderful mentor.

I realized that this was the opportunity I had been looking for. If I hopped in the pool and people saw me swimming, they would know that despite my blindness, nothing had changed.

The next morning, I asked my mom to drive me to the pool, just like when I was fifteen years old. When we walked onto the pool deck, my mom noted that Fred was sitting on the same white patio chair and wearing the same old Cape May Beach Patrol jacket that he wore when I was a teenager. He smiled and greeted us, but before long, got strictly down to business.

Fred handed me a swim mask, and told me that I should wear the mask instead of goggles because my eyes were still so sensitive. He also explained that he had set up a lane with two foam noodles at each end, which he had strung across the lane just in front of the wall. This way, I would know when I was about to reach the wall, and could turn around without hitting my head.

Fred also handed me a new swimsuit.

"Get in the locker room and put this on," he said. "I don't have all day!"

I smiled. Indeed, nothing had changed.

As I eased myself into the chilly water, the rest of the world floated away. I felt a freedom that I hadn't felt in a long time. I felt free from the burdens of gravity, my personal expectations, my daily struggles to adapt to blindness, and from my need for a guide. As I submerged, all that was left was me and the water. Since I had swum through this pool so many times, I was able to draw a vivid mental image of my surroundings.

Even though I was blind, I could "see" the black line on the bottom of the pool. I could also "see" that the blue and red plastic rings on the lane lines were to my right and left. I pushed off the wall, and stretched my body into a streamline. After a few kicks, I breached the surface, and slowly began stroke after stroke.

I began counting in order to perceive my distance across the pool. As I reached out on my fourteenth stroke, my head nudged against the foam noodle, and just beyond it, my hand found the lip of the opposing wall. I swung my legs around and pushed off in the other direction.

While I had already resolved that nothing about me had changed, I don't think I actually believed it until that exact moment. In the pool, I truly felt like my old self. As my coach, my mom, and others watched me swim that morning, I think they felt it, too.

Tap, advance.

18

My Country Calls Back

Once again, the beautiful beaches of my dreams were replaced with darkness when I woke up in a lonely hospital bed. This time, I was in Augusta, Georgia, after successfully completing my five-week stay at the VA facility in Tampa.

My physical wounds had fully and finally healed during my Florida stint. The large lacerations across my face were now tight pink scars, the bone in my hand had mended, and I had temporary, prosthetic eyes, which were stretching my damaged eyelids in preparation for more permanent prosthetics that I would receive later on.

The doctors had also determined that I should be transferred to a VA facility where I could receive full-time instruction from a staff that specialized in helping veterans with visual impairments adjust to the challenges of life without vision. Think "Hogwarts," but for blind people instead of wizards. There were a number of such facilities across the country, but the closest to home was Augusta.

I rolled out of bed and felt my way across the room until I found the doorknob to my bathroom. The sink was located in the back right corner, which I was able to find with little trouble. From a small toiletry case that I kept on a ledge above the mirror, I removed my toothbrush and a tube of toothpaste. I unscrewed the toothpaste cap and did my best to line the nozzle up with the end of my toothbrush.

Several failed attempts at this process yielded a large mess of toothpaste in the bottom of the sink, and left me starting off the day in frustration. I used to be capable of removing a blasting cap from a complex explosive device, whether it was buried beneath the sands of Afghanistan or hidden in the ocean's depths. Now, I was struggling with the cap of a toothpaste tube.

Fuming, I used my fingers to scrape up some spilled toothpaste and angrily smeared it on the end of the toothbrush. I then jammed the toothbrush in my mouth and took out some pent-up frustration on my gums.

Just outside the bathroom door stood a tall locker where I kept my belongings. I only had a few personal items with me in Augusta, as most of my things were either in storage at my base in Virginia Beach, or still in Afghanistan. Fortunately, my family members had taken me to a mall when I was hospitalized in Florida to pick up a few articles of clothing. Those new garments were neatly arranged in front of me inside my closet, which now resembled my perfectly put together "plebe summer" closet at the Naval Academy.

To accomplish this feat, which was no easy task in the early stages of blindness, I was helped by a small handheld device that resembled a TV remote. The device told me the color of each of my shirts, which helped me carefully arrange them, as well as my socks and even my underwear, in a systematic "dark to light, left to right" order. This way, I would always know what color shirt I was grabbing.

I selected a black t-shirt from the left, and slid on my only pair of jeans. I zipped up my only fleece jacket, and tucked a pair of gloves into my back pocket. I slipped on a pair of sneakers, grabbed my cane, and tapped my way to the door. Outside, I turned right, and followed the right side of the hallway past four doors, then turned ninety degrees to cross the hallway.

As my cane smacked the nurse's station, I issued a cordial "good morning!" to the two nurses sitting behind the chest-high counter. After a moment or two of small talk, I followed the curved counter until it ended, then tapped forward until I found the right side of the hallway that led out of our ward. I followed this wall past the nurse administrator's office, which always smelled like a Yankee Candle.

Next, I felt the metal lip below a set of fire doors as I left the ward before feeling the hallway broaden ever so slightly. I continued following the right side of the hallway a few more paces until a T intersection with a much larger hallway. I turned right and continued following the right side until passing a set of drinking fountains.

Just past the fountains, I took another ninety-degree turn, crossing the larger hallway to a bank of elevators. I felt along the wall in between the two elevators on the left-hand side of the alcove until I found the "up" and "down" buttons. I pressed the down button a few times to ensure that I activated it, and then listened intently as I waited.

I heard a "ding!" from behind me and slightly to the right, then the swish of the sliding elevator doors. With my cane angled in front of me, I whirled around and darted toward the sounds.

When I first arrived in Augusta, it had taken me a while to figure out how to follow the sound of the opening elevator, and in the process, I had missed quite a few rides. Just before missing this one, though, I slid my cane and outstretched hand in between the closing elevator doors, causing them to reopen.

Once inside, I felt along the left-hand side of the front wall to locate the bank of floor buttons. I was learning Braille, but in the meantime, I found it much easier to feel for the shape of the letters, numbers, and symbols next to each button. I felt around for a while until I touched a five-pointed star shape raised out of the panel next to the number one. I pressed the associated button, and felt the elevator floor dip. When the doors subsequently slid open at my desired floor, I stepped out and took an immediate left turn. I followed the left hand wall just a pace or two, then squared off and crossed the hallway.

I would eventually turn left, so it would have been easier to follow the left wall, but at the same time, I didn't want to be walking the wrong way down the hallway. It was amazing—and a bit disappointing—how little attention was often paid by those with functioning eyes. On previous treks down this hallway, I had been bumped into a number of times, and on one occasion, accidentally knocked someone over.

Across the hallway, I turned left, and subsequently followed the right-hand side of the wide hallway. It was early, so not many hospital employees had arrived to work. I took advantage of the silence by stepping just to the left of the wall, and then following it by listening for the echo of my cane taps instead of actually tapping the wall. This sort of echolocation is used by the blind to perceive their surroundings and navigate, but I was terrible at it, and needed as much practice as possible.

From the opposite direction, I then heard someone—most likely a janitor or facilities manager, judging by the thick ring of jingling keys—coming down the hallway. As the person approached, I darted back over to the wall to ensure that I was in the right spot.

Soon, I passed another metal rim at a new set of fire doors, and began listening for the space to open up on the left side.

After about ten or so paces, I heard an air conditioning vent blowing from a deeper, open spot on the left side of the hallway, indicating the presence of a smaller passageway moving off to the left. I squared off and again crossed the hallway, finding the right-hand side of the offshoot passageway, following it until I passed another set of fire doors, and then slid across the narrow passageway to the left-hand side. Once on the left, I began dragging my cane along the bottom of the wall and looking for the next doorway. Within a pace or two, my cane struck a metal door frame with a gratifying sound: "tin!"

"You did it!" cheered a mobility instructor named Lauren (celebrity look-alike: a short-haired Anne Hathaway) from inside her small office, where she was typing at her computer while seated in the far corner of the room, as far as I could tell.

While seemingly insignificant to others at first glance, this lengthy hospital trek had marked my first mobility test. Lauren and I had gone over that route during the previous few days; just a few short weeks earlier, I had been afraid to traverse my own hospital room to the bathroom, let alone tap across an open hallway. Now, I was able to find my way across an entire hospital and pick out an exact office.

From the doorway, I beamed with pride. Lauren stood up to give me a hug, and then offered that we go to the coffee shop down the hall to celebrate.

"I'll lead the way!" I proclaimed.

LATER THAT DAY, I sat facing a computer screen that I couldn't see, but could hear. Amazingly, a voice was relaying each key that I typed.

Seated next to me was Ron (celebrity look-alike: Woody Harrelson, with a mustache), my computer instructor, who was also blind.

"Isn't it neat to talk to a computer?" I typed into a blank document as Ron and I both listened.

Ron then instructed me to save the document to the desktop. He walked me through the audible menu screens, while giving me a few keyboard shortcuts to make the arduous process a bit quicker. Ron then instructed me to close the word processing program and find the document that I had just saved on the desktop. We both smiled as I found it.

"Isn't it neat to talk to a computer?" the computer said just as I opened the document, which caused both Ron and me to laugh.

In that humorous moment, I think that it also became clear to Ron that operating the computer wasn't going to be the biggest challenge I faced while adjusting to being blind.

I heard a jingle of dog tags as Ron reached down to scratch the ears of his guide dog, a blonde lab named Mara.

"So Brad, what has been the hardest adjustment for you?" Ron asked while petting his trusted guide dog.

After thinking about his question for a moment, it didn't take me very long to recall the toothpaste incident. As I relayed my embarrassing struggle, Ron just laughed, having clearly faced the same dilemma in his own early days of blindness.

"Well that one's easy," Ron said. "You just squirt the toothpaste directly into your mouth … no fuss, no mess!"

I joined in his laughter. He was right … it's so simple!

In that moment, I realized the way I would succeed as a blind man was to embrace each new challenge with an open mind, and most importantly, patience. I would have to think outside the box to solve problems and adapt to each new situation, much like when I was learning to disable enemy IEDs.

Over time, I would adjust to my new lifestyle, but every day would hold new challenges. As always, constant challenge would be a way of life, but like everyone had been teaching me at the various hospitals I had stayed in since my injury, the only way I would succeed was—in the words of the blind Army captain, Ivan—"one step at a time."

MARIMBAS ERUPTED FROM MY iPhone as the voice of Siri indicated that I had an incoming call from a number with a Colorado Springs area code. I tapped the screen and held the phone to my ear, but before I could say much more than "hello," an excited voice introduced himself as Rich Cardillo, the Military Outreach Coordinator for the United States Association of Blind Athletes (USABA).

Rich explained that it was his job to seek out veterans and service members who suffered from vision loss, and to provide them with resources that would push them toward getting involved in adaptive sports. He added that my information had come across his desk, and he was both aware of and excited about my sports background.

It may have been the poor cell phone connection, but it seemed to me that Rich was genuinely excited about the opportunities that losing my vision had opened up for me. Rich's enthusiastic approach was a far cry from what I had become accustomed to, and it was actually quite refreshing not to be pitied.

My mind started to wander as I heard Rich say something about the "Paralympics" and the "United States Association of Blind Athletes."

The Paralympics? What's that? Is that like the Special Olympics? My mind continued to race.

Association of what? Blind athletes? We have those? What sports do they play? Arm wrestling? I don't suppose you would need your eyes for that …

I stopped Rich and asked him to back up for a second. He explained that it was the mission of the USABA to provide resources and establish programs for all those with visual impairments to get involved in sports. That meant real sports, like running, cycling, swimming, judo, and even a sport called "goalball" that is played exclusively by blind athletes. My antenna went up even further when I heard the word "swimming." Not only had I competed at the Division I level, but my former swim coach, Fred Lewis, had already helped teach me how to swim while blind.

Rich went on to explain that there was an event called the Paralympics, which is modeled after the Olympic Games and different from the Special Olympics, which is designed for those with cognitive impairments.

Every four years, after the Olympic torch is extinguished, the Paralympic torch is lit. In the same immense Olympic venues, athletes with physical disabilities like missing limbs, paralysis, or blindness compete in sports that are adapted from the Olympics. As Rich explained, I was more than likely eligible to compete in the Paralympics in the S11 classification, which consists of athletes who are all completely blind.

The next Paralympic Games were set for London in 2012. Given my background in swimming, Rich believed that I had a good chance of making Team USA. I suppose I was lucky to have suffered my injury so close to a Paralympic year.

Rich explained that if I had any interest whatsoever in competing, I needed to immediately begin the process of applying for eligibility. I would also need to swim in a competition very soon in order to meet the various qualifying standards.

Even though I was energized by Rich's enthusiasm, seeds of doubt nevertheless crept into my head. I told Rich that I was interested, but also not quite sure what to make of this brand-new information. I also admitted that I was still very uncertain about my overall future, which made trying out for the Paralympics at this early stage of blindness seem difficult, if not impossible. Still, I thanked Rich and told him that I would consider his proposal and that I would be in touch. I was late for computer class with Ron, so I quickly grabbed my cane and tapped my way out.

Rich called back a few days later and asked if I had considered the Paralympics, to which I admitted that I had not. I told him that I had been busy with the requirements of my rehab, and hadn't gotten a chance to sit down and give it some thought. Honestly, I had thought about it a little, but between the mobility training, computer classes, and adjusting to the huge demands of my new reality, I didn't feel like I had the bandwidth to add something else, especially athletic competition.

Swimming in Florida had been a lot of fun. It was also a nice escape from the early confusion and frustration I felt after being blinded at such a young age. Still, I needed to focus on learning the skills that would help me potentially go back to school, get a job, and help me find a new, promising career that I could manage and eventually succeed in despite my vision loss. I didn't see how swim training and competing could help me with that.

I didn't want to say this to Rich, though, as he seemed so excited about the idea of me benefiting from competitive sports. He was able to sense my trepidation, however, prompting him to set about selling me on the idea.

To my surprise, Rich explained that he had already worked out all the details on my behalf. He had filled out all the paperwork and just needed me to sign in a few places. Amazingly, Rich also found a local coach who knew a great deal about Paralympic swimming.

As my excitement grew, Rich said that he could arrange it with the hospital staff so that I would be allowed to leave for two hours after lunch—three days a week—to attend swimming practices. Rich could also work it out so that I could take leave at the end of February to fly to the Olympic Training Center in Colorado Springs, where I could swim in my first meet as a blind athlete. He could make all these incredible things happen thanks to funding that was available from the USABA.

I was shocked by how much effort Rich had put forth on my behalf. He had truly invested himself in me, and I was deeply touched.

Even if I didn't come close to making the Paralympic team, Rich had arranged things so that the effort required from me was mostly minimal. At the same time, I found the prospect of sneaking out of the hospital and into the water, where I had felt so comfortable since childhood, to be quite attractive. Plus, what if I actually had a chance to be good at it? Rich had succeeded in convincing me to give this seemingly crazy idea a shot.

"NOW LISTEN HERE, BRADLEY," said Fred Lambeck, my new swim coach (celebrity look-alike: Patrick Stewart with a southern accent). "This here is a tapper."

It sounded more like "tappa" because of Fred's thick accent, but I understood him just fine. After placing one of my folding canes in my hand, he demonstrated how he had just taped a tennis ball at the end. Fred had cut a small hole in the tennis ball and jammed the tip of the cane through the hole before securing it with duct tape.

My family and I had spent some time speculating as to how a blind swimmer might execute a proper turn in competition, and while doing so, we had come up with quite a few crazy ideas. We tossed around everything from directed sprinkler systems to portable sonar arrays until someone had the brilliant idea to simply search YouTube for a video of blind swimmers actually competing in the Paralympic Games.

My brother narrated a short video clip for me. He said that blind swimmers dove off a block and began sprinting across the pool. At the end stood a line of coaches and teammates—one per swimmer—who were all getting ready with long poles. As each swimmer approached the wall, the "tappers," one by one, reached out and smacked the oncoming blind swimmer on the back or even the head with the long pole.

"That's it?" I asked.

A few days later, Fred gave me an even more detailed demonstration. He told me to swim into the wall, slowly at first, and he'd tap me when I should turn. I did so, and after a few strokes, I felt the tennis ball hit my shoulder blade. I tucked my chin to my chest, pressed my shoulders down, and kicked my legs over my head, just like I had learned so many years ago in Florida. My body rotated one hundred eighty degrees, and my feet landed perfectly on the wall.

Underwater, I smiled as I pushed off into a streamline and started swimming the other direction. It was really that simple. Just like the darn toothpaste.

EVERY OTHER DAY FOR about six weeks, Coach Fred Lambeck would pick me up at the hospital for practice. One day in late February 2012, though, Fred drove us to Augusta's tiny airport instead of the local YMCA.

Together, Fred and I flew to Chicago, and then to Colorado Springs. The next day, Fred escorted me out on to the deck of the US Olympic Training Center's pool. Never in my wildest dreams—or post-injury hallucinations—did I think I would end up here.

The pool deck was a chaotic mix of sounds, ranging from coaches chatting excitedly about the upcoming Paralympics to officials testing the loudspeaker and starting buzzer. The volume of the noise was slightly unsettling, even though at the same time, I was comforted by the familiar sounds and smells of a swim meet. Even if I was a little uncomfortable at first, I knew that this was where I belonged.

After an official cleared the pool, an announcer welcomed us to the annual Jimi Flowers swim meet. The announcer called the arena to attention for the playing of the national anthem, and soon after, the day's first race was underway.

Fred guided me over to the starting block area and told me that I would be swimming in the first heat of the next event, which was nine races away. Fred then left me there so that he could be ready to tap me with the tennis ball at the other end of the pool.

After eight heats, I started inching forward. A swim meet volunteer noticed me feeling for the block, and kindly escorted me to my lane. After thanking her, I began stretching and warming up, just like I had before my races as a Naval Academy midshipman. I put on my goggles, then a cap emblazoned with the Navy "N star" on one side and the American flag on the other. Finally, the referee called my heat to the block.

"Take your marks!" he commanded, and a second later, the buzzer started the clock.

I leapt off the blocks and swam as fast as I could across the pool. At the other side, Fred slapped me in the back with the tapper, and I reached out my hand for the timing pad.

I swam to the side of the pool and exited at a ladder, where Fred was waiting for me. He didn't make any effort to hide his excitement when he told me that my time was 26.9 seconds, which had been the world's fifth-fastest recorded time for a blind swimmer.

Most importantly, it was also fast enough to earn me a spot on the US Paralympic National team. If I could go that fast again in June during the Paralympic Trials, I would be named to Team USA's roster in London.

BACK IN AUGUSTA A few days later, marimbas once again chimed from my phone. This time, Siri informed me that it was a number with a District of Columbia area code.

The voice on the other end of the line belonged to Guy Filippelli, a West Point graduate who had left the Army a few years prior to begin a lucrative career as an entrepreneur. After introducing himself, Guy said that he'd just started a non-profit called the COMMIT Foundation, with an aim of helping veterans like me transition into meaningful and fulfilling post-military careers in the private sector.

Guy offered me an internship with his newest company, Red Owl Analytics, where I could learn all the skills I would need to begin a new career in the corporate world. I was very excited about this amazing opportunity. After quickly accepting the internship, I thanked Guy profusely.

Immediately after I hung up the phone, however, I found myself conflicted. What about the Paralympics? Could I possibly manage the onset of a new career, while at the same time dedicating the necessary time and effort to training with the hopes of going to London?

That question burned inside my brain and ate away at me for the following few days. I spoke at length about the issue with my family, and in the end, I decided that doing the internship, on top of Paralympic training, would be far too overwhelming.

Blindness was still so new, and while I wanted to get going as quickly as possible, I didn't want to get myself into a situation where I had bitten off more than I could chew. I had to pick one or the other, and I would then allot my full focus and effort to that one endeavor.

After going back and forth on my decision again and again, in the end, I decided that because the Paralympics were coming up in

September, I would throw my full focus towards swimming. I would then attempt to re-address the internship in the fall.

I dialed Guy's phone number and took a deep breath. I was not looking forward to reneging on my acceptance of the internship. Guy had been so kind to go out of his way to help me, and I didn't like that I now had to say "no thanks."

When Guy answered, I rambled through an explanation of my previous day's thoughts, concluding that I had no choice but to turn down his generous offer. Guy laughed, and asked that I not give up on him so fast. He said that he was going to work on a few things, then call me back.

As promised, I got a call back, and Guy explained that his friend Anne Meree had done some digging, and they had developed a plan where I could work as an intern at Red Owl while training at the same time. My prosthetic eyes widened as Guy outlined a plan where I would live in a downtown Baltimore apartment provided by the COMMIT Foundation.

I would work with Guy a short distance away, and then someone from Red Owl or COMMIT would drive me to Loyola University once a day for practice. There, I would train with Brian Loeffler; the head coach of Loyola's swimming and diving program. Brian had also coached the only recent blind athlete to compete in the Paralympics for Team USA, who had been a student at Loyola. Brian had been his coach and mentor for the previous four years.

Through this process, Brian had proven to be an invaluable resource to the US Paralympic program, especially after offering his coaching, mentorship, and assistance to several more Paralympic athletes. Recognizing his efforts and expertise, the US Paralympic program had named Brian to the roster of coaches that would be going to London.

My jaw dropped as Guy's plan materialized in my head. I was in awe of his generosity, as well as in awe of the fact that an elite coach like Brian just happened to be in Baltimore, where this internship opportunity was. I was dumbfounded by the serendipity of this circumstance.

Guy seemed to beam with pride as he explained the logistics behind this plan, and once again, I had no choice but to accept his amazing offer, while of course thanking him profusely.

After hanging up, though, I was stricken with fear that maybe I was overextending myself. Was I taking on too much?

I found my imagination taking me back to Weeki Wachee Springs, where my dad had asked if I was afraid of the imaginary monsters below. Even though I had been afraid, I proclaimed that I wasn't, and was subsequently rewarded when I conquered my fears and stole a shell from the bottom.

I didn't want to be petrified by my fears. Laid out in front of me was a golden opportunity, and I would be a fool not to take advantage of it.

19

A Golden Opportunity

In front of a sold-out Major League Baseball opening weekend crowd, my sister guided me to the mound at Tropicana Field in my hometown of St. Petersburg. Somehow, the Tampa Bay Rays had caught wind of my story, and upon my release from the hospital in Augusta, I was invited to throw out the first pitch at a home game against the New York Yankees.

For a few hours prior to the game, I had practiced throwing sixty-foot pitches to my friend Bob, and after a while, we thought I had it down. As excited as I was to have the once-in-a-lifetime opportunity to throw out a pitch at the beloved "Trop," I didn't want that once-in-a-lifetime opportunity to end up on SportsCenter's Friday funnies, or on blooper reels for years to come.

Immediately following the national anthem, my sister and I took the field, and Elyse proceeded to line me up towards home plate. The plan was for Rays middle reliever Kyle Farnsworth to stand behind home plate and smack his glove loud enough so that I would know where to throw the baseball. What we had failed to anticipate, though, was the sold-out crowd's reaction to what was playing on the scoreboard: my story.

The announcer read a short bio, after which a few photos of me popped up on the big screen behind me in left field. Upon realization that I was a blinded Afghanistan war veteran, the crowd collectively got on their feet and began cheering. I was, of course, immensely moved by the touching gesture. At the same time, though, I became instantly worried that I might not be able to hear Farnsworth's glove, and thus, would have no idea where to throw the ball.

After a few moments of hesitation, it became clear that I wouldn't be able to hear anything over the cheering crowd. I barely heard my sister, who was standing right next to me, yell, "Just go for it, Brad!"

I shrugged my shoulders and resigned myself to the sports hall of shame. Without thinking any further, I wound up and chucked the ball towards my best guess of where home plate might be. The next few moments felt like an eternity as I waited for the ball to sail toward the dugout, the stands, or perhaps even the mascot's head.

To my amazement, the crowd of thirty thousand fans roared! Amid my confusion, my sister excitedly reported that I had in fact thrown a perfect strike directly across home plate.

Elated, I threw my fists in the air in a "V for victory" pose. In response, the crowd cheered even louder. What a moment.

THE NEXT DAY, my friend Bob, who had helped me prepare for the first pitch, and his wife Ali joined my family for a big Sunday brunch celebration. All of us were on a high from the baseball game, and the friendly company and delicious food made the day even better.

As soon as the plates were cleared, though, it was time for Mom and me to head to the airport. Guy and Anne Meree had everything set up in Baltimore for me to begin work at Red Owl, and to start training for the Paralympic Trials with Brian at Loyola.

My mom stayed the week and helped me acclimate to yet another new environment. She helped me outfit and organize my new apartment, figure out routes to the grocery store across the street, and most importantly, helped me figure out how to order sandwiches from Jimmy John's. My mom also went with me to my new office, and accompanied me to the pool to meet Brian for the first time. She helped me figure out that Guy's celebrity look-alike is Jeff Daniels with dark hair, Anne Meree is Molly Shannon with blonde hair, her husband Les is Michael J. Fox, while Brian is Drew Carey, albeit with longer, darker hair.

Content that I had a good setup, my mom left the following weekend. Early Monday morning, Les picked me up to take me to practice with Brian, and then gave me a ride back downtown for work. Les was also a West Point graduate and an Army Ranger who had recently gotten out of the service. We rapidly became good friends while spending a great deal of quality time together on the way to and from practice and work.

Over the previous few months, I had temporarily lived in Afghanistan, Germany, Bethesda, Tampa, and Augusta, but for whatever reason, the early rhythm that I established in Baltimore felt more permanent.

The learning curve at Red Owl, where I was starting my new internship, was steep. The good news, though, was that I found the challenge exhilarating. Admittedly, I sometimes fell asleep at my computer after becoming exhausted from the workload. But within a few weeks, I began to feel more comfortable than I had been since the days before my injury.

After a few weeks of this routine, it was time to head to the Paralympic Trials in Bismarck, North Dakota. Brian and I flew together from Baltimore, and my brother Mitch was able to take some time off from pharmacy school to meet us there.

Based on my experience as a collegiate distance swimmer, Brian and I suspected that my best event would be the four hundred meter (400m) race. Still, neither of us truly had a firm idea of what my potential was so soon after my injury. We agreed that I would swim all seven events available on the program: 50m freestyle, 100m freestyle, 400m freestyle, 100m butterfly, 100m backstroke, 100m breaststroke, and a 200m individual medley.

Luckily, my first race was the 400m, and with Brian on the start end and Mitch tapping on the other side, I dove in and swam a 4:39.52, which was the fastest time by a blind swimmer in 2012. In the finals that evening, I swam a 4:35.62, solidifying my place atop the world rankings list.

Brian seemed convinced that would be enough to earn me a spot on the team, but I'm not one to leave anything to chance. Besides, I was still unsure what I might be capable of in the other races, and wanted to challenge myself to do my very best.

The following day, I swam the 100m freestyle in another top-ranked time, as well as a top-three finish in the 100m butterfly. Over the next few days, I managed to raise my ranking in the 50m freestyle from fifth to third. While the rest of my swims were none too impressive, I still managed to squeak into the top eight in each race.

After the final competition, all athletes were invited to a ceremony in a nearby auditorium, where the London roster would officially be announced. Dramatically, one by one, athletes were selected based on their performance at the trials as compared to the rest of the world's most recent performances. Brian had assured me that my performance had been enough, but to me, nothing was ever official until it was official.

Mitch sat next to me while athlete after athlete was announced; first the women's team, then the men's, in alphabetical order. I knew that if "Snyder" was on the list, it would be near the end, but it was still a bit gut-wrenching to hear name after name called without hearing mine.

Just as I began to second-guess my performance, "Brad Snyder" was announced. All the athletes and coaches in the small auditorium stood and applauded as Mitch and I walked up onto the stage to join Team USA for the first time.

Even though I had trained for this moment, I couldn't believe it had actually happened. Amid so much good fortune, the only thing I wished was that I could have seen the looks on everyone's faces. I just wanted to look into their eyes to say "thank you," because without so many people helping and believing in me, I never would have made it.

A FEW WEEKS LATER, Les dropped me off at Loyola University's Fitness and Aquatic Center. I caned my way inside, changed into my swimsuit, and then found my way out onto the pool deck. I followed a pool grate on the deck to my lane, felt out where the edge of the pool was, then began stretching and visualizing like I always did before practice.

After a few minutes, Brian came out of his office with a piece of paper in his hand, and told me that he had the schedule of events for the London Paralympics. We decided to take a moment to review the order so that we might visualize and train for the specific schedule.

With top eight rankings in all seven events, Brian and I reasoned that I should swim the full program. Neither of us was quite sure how I would fare, but as intense competitors, I think we both dreamed of medal-winning finishes across the board.

Brian began by saying that the first event would be the 100m freestyle, and while it wasn't my best, it would still be a great opportunity to get in some good racing early on in the Paralympics. If I swam well, it would send a message that I was ready to go, and would lay a solid foundation for the many other races that would follow.

Mental momentum is big in our sport, and it's important to ride your highs and forget about your lows. Swimming the 100m freestyle would also be a great chance to get used to the procedure of checking in early, going through the ready room, and then racing in front of such a big crowd. This would be a major departure from anything I had previously experienced in my swimming career.

Brian went on to say that after the 100m freestyle, I would swim the 100m breaststroke, then after a day off, compete in the 50m freestyle. While my ranking in the 50m was only fifth, the difference between there and the gold medal was only a half a second. We surmised that I had a realistic shot at potentially winning that event.

Brian got quiet for a moment as—I assumed—his eyes made their way down to the next few lines.

"On the seventh of September, you'll swim the 400m freestyle …" Brian said with a slight quiver in his voice.

I got goosebumps. September 7 would mark one year to the day since I stepped on the IED in Afghanistan.

Soon, the reality that I would have the opportunity to don a new uniform—reading "Team USA"—began to set in. In London, I would indeed get a golden opportunity to represent my country and the US Navy. I knew I had moved to Baltimore for an important reason, but I could never have dreamed of this.

20

Alive Day

Leading up to the 2012 Paralympic Games, my family and friends searched the Internet for videos of a Spanish swimmer named Enhamed Enhamed, who had ruled the pool against all other blind swimmers at the 2008 Paralympics in Beijing. He had won all three freestyle events while also setting a world record in the 100m butterfly, for a total of four gold medals.

Even though I had never met Enhamed (let alone raced against him), my family and friends made him out to be some sort of fierce rival. They also spoke of a Chinese swimmer named Yang Bozun, who had clearly improved in the four years since squaring off against Enhamed in Beijing. Surely, both athletes would serve as stiff competition in my quest for a gold medal.

Once we got to London, Brian would be on the lookout for Yang and Enhamed to evaluate how well each was swimming. While both were in great physical shape, along with being taller than me, it seemed that Enhamed had a slight advantage.

We arrived in the Olympic village in London, where both Olympians and Paralympians would live—a few days before the torch was lit. The time we spent in the village flew by, and before I knew it, I was walking to the blocks for my first race, the 100m freestyle.

Admittedly, the large crowd managed to get inside my head, and my adrenaline started pumping. In fact, I felt the same way as when I approached the IED that Alaska found at the entrance of Building Thirty-Eight.

Just as when I was in Afghanistan, however, a sense of calm washed over me just prior to the race. I tore up and back in 57.18 seconds, which set a new Paralympic record. I went into the finals seeded first, having made the statement we had set out to make. I was ready to race, and I was ready to race fast.

In the finals that night, I dove off and rapidly fell behind the lead pack, including both Enhamed and Bonsun. I made up a little ground on the turn, and then—only about ten meters off the wall on the return leg—I caught the pack. About halfway back, Bonsun and I started to edge out ahead of the field.

With only fifteen meters to go, Bonsun and I had a healthy lead, but it was too close to call between the two of us. With about five meters left, Bonsun grazed the lane line, which caused him to lose precious speed. I surged forward, and slapped the timing pad for my first gold medal!

It was an immense relief, and an altogether great feeling to come out of the gates so strong. While we had a long week of racing ahead, culminating with the 400m freestyle on the anniversary of my injury, the first win gave me a healthy amount of optimism. No matter what transpired the rest of the way, I would be going home having accomplished something that was unthinkable as I hallucinated in a hospital bed a few short months earlier.

The 100m breaststroke came and went, and my performance was unremarkable. I have never felt comfortable swimming that stroke, and despite over a decade's worth of effort, I still just haven't figured it out.

Preliminary rounds for the 50m freestyle were much more exciting. I dropped a little bit of time in the morning heat, and had earned the second seed going into finals, coming in just a fraction of a second behind Yang. Knowing that a potential crash at full speed might dramatically alter the outcome of the race, Brian and I had our sights set on another gold medal.

In the finals, I tore down the middle of the lane better than ever before and touched the wall in 25.9 seconds, which was my fastest time by almost half a second, and only a few hundredths off the world record. That is, the previous world record, as Yang had touched the wall ahead of me in 25.27 seconds, blowing the previous world record of 25.88 out of the water.

Later in the waiting room prior to our medal presentation, I chatted with Yang and Enhamed. While my family and I had tried to make them out to be fierce villainous rivals, it turned out that they were both really nice guys. Despite the language barrier, the three of us managed to express a mutual respect for one another, and at the same time, commiserated over the struggles of being blind in such a visual world.

It immediately struck me how just a few moments earlier, all three of us had been competitors in a great arena. Now, we were all just blind guys trying to make our way through our adapted lives. Through those key moments and our friendly exchange, I came to understand the power and magic of the Paralympic movement.

JUST BEFORE THE PARALYMPICS, a sports reporter had asked me a pointed question.

"Lieutenant Snyder, are you nervous to compete in the Paralympics for the first time?" she said.

"No," I arrogantly replied without thinking my answer through. "I spent half of last year conducting assault operations and defusing bombs in Afghanistan. How hard could the Paralympics be?"

The fallacy of this statement was clear to me in the tense moments immediately prior to competing in the finals heat of the S11 400m freestyle at the Games in London. A gold medal in men's swimming was on the line.

At major international competitions such as this one, athletes are required to show up and check-in well in advance of their scheduled race in order to be inspected and officially ushered to their assigned lanes. The ensuing wait offers ample opportunity for athletes to reaffirm their preparations and establish a mindset for victory, or allows doubts and distractions to devastate their psyches.

After an International Paralympic Committee (IPC) official thoroughly inspected my swim cap, goggles, and racing suit to ensure my gear was in accordance with the plethora of peculiar international rules, he ushered me to a row of eight chairs. There are multiple sets of chairs, each for a scheduled heat for the evening's finals session. Athletes were to wait in this area like actors waiting before a pivotal scene, while a swarm of volunteers buzzed around the room frenetically ensuring the event went off without a hitch.

The official tapped on the fourth chair from the right, which would be my seat. My time from the preliminary heats had been a 4:33.70, earning me the top seed for the S11 finals heat.

The air in the room was chilly, and there was little sound other than the shuffling of other athletes getting inspected and finding their way to their assigned chairs. Though I couldn't see him, I knew that Brian was patiently waiting somewhere against the wall across from me. I was the first from my classification to sit down, so as I stretched, I could feel the other competitors, including Enhamed and Yang, fill in around me.

All of us were focused on the race, so there would be no chatting with my rivals. Then, the air conditioning vent above me clicked on, which gave me goose bumps, similar to the moment when I found out that this race would be held on such a significant date.

I pulled the hood of my sweatshirt over my head. I put in earbuds, and began blasting rock music in an attempt to drown out my nerves. I needed to visualize my race.

Those cocky remarks I made to the reporter had been echoing through my head over the past few days. I was ashamed by how I underestimated the gravity of this experience. I had been in awe walking around in the Olympic village and listening to athletes from all over the world chat excitedly about competing in their respective sports. I had been amazed by the immensity of the cafeteria and all of the living accommodations for the athletes.

Most of all, I had been overwhelmed by the response of a sold-out crowd of over eighteen thousand international spectators in an arena surrounding a pool. Each and every fan seemed genuinely excited to watch my sport: swimming.

As I tried to focus on the biggest race of my life, I thought about some of my previous swimming experiences. From the summer swim league when I was a kid to the NCAA Division I Eastern Intercollegiate Swimming League Championships when I was at Navy, I don't think I had ever swum in front of more than a few hundred people, most of whom were family and friends.

In London, though, the stands were packed with general spectators and fans of the Paralympic movement, all of whom were there to support the best disabled athletes in the world. They rooted on hometown heroes and international athletes alike.

When I walked out for my first race in London a few days earlier, I had heard a sell-out crowd of people from all over the world cheering for me. For me! I didn't know more than a dozen or so people in the stands, but the sound of the cheers was nearly deafening and entirely humbling. This instilled in me an acute awareness of nerves not unlike the ones I had experienced on the battlefields of Afghanistan. It made me really nervous.

Leading up to my first race, my hands had shook, my heart rate was out of control, and it felt like the butterflies in my stomach were engaged in intense combat. I remember removing my earbuds and needing to do a few deep breathing exercises to gain control of my heart rate. After calming down, I had been surprisingly able to set that Paralympic record.

The 400m race would be different, though. It was September 7, 2012, which was just another date on the calendar for many, but not for me. The seventh of September is my "Alive Day."

Many wounded veterans refer to the day they suffered their combat wounds as their Alive Day because we realize how close we came to dying. For most of us, that day marks being given a tremendous gift, much like our birthdays. While we come back from Afghanistan or Iraq with less than we left with, the important part is that we came back. September 7, 2012, was my very first Alive Day.

Just one year prior, I had been clearing my way across one of the most dangerous places on earth, rife with buried explosive devices and Taliban fighters. Somehow, I had lived through an explosion, but had forever lost the use of my eyes.

Now I was in London at the Paralympic Games. I was wearing a new uniform, having traded in my US Navy fatigues for Team USA warm-ups. In a few moments, I would compete for my country on international soil in front of a screaming crowd. Having earned the top seed, I didn't want to let anyone down.

On the outside, that may seem like a great potential sports story, but as I tapped my foot nervously in the "ready room" just before the race, that story was terrifying. It was terrifying because it hadn't come true. Before I had returned to the pool that evening, I had received hundreds of Facebook messages, posts, and tweets from friends, family, and strangers from all over the world. All of those people would presumably be watching and hoping to see something special.

While I was in the ready room, I thought of all those people about to watch the race, whether at home with their families or in small huts while deployed to Afghanistan. In that moment, I felt the collective expectations of all those people weighing heavily on my shoulders.

What would happen if I screwed this up? What if I false started? What if I was disqualified? What if I dove in and just didn't have anything left? What if I crashed?

I caught that negative spiral before it could do any real damage. I realized that it did me no good to "what if?" myself. Doubt is a tricky demon, and it can wiggle its way into your head wherever it can find a crack. You can protect yourself with preparation and positivity, and if you believe in yourself with enough conviction, you can shut out those doubts. I decided in that moment—in the ready room—that if I focused on the outcome that I wanted hard enough, then I could make it come true. I was prepared, I was strong, I was ready, and I was determined to make this incredible story a reality.

I suddenly felt a rising tide of adrenaline. Over and over in my head, I saw myself diving off the blocks and flawlessly executing lap after lap with smooth, effortless speed.

As each heat was announced, started, and completed, I would advance into a new set of chairs. There are probably six or so sets of chairs, so every few minutes, Brian would tap my shoulder and escort me to a new chair, bringing me closer and closer to the pool deck and all eighteen thousand fans. Their expectations, which were collectively voiced in a cacophony of sound waves that crashed against my consciousness, caused me to clench my jaw, steel my resolve, and step confidently forward.

In the last set of chairs, I set my goggles over my prosthetic eyes while checking that my swim cap was tight on my head. Once again, I pulled my hood over my head and hid my stoic face in the shadows.

A different IPC official said that we were the next heat to be announced, and that we should line up at the doorway to the pool deck. A loud and booming voice echoed through the arena, just slightly louder than the crowd's cheers, announcing, "Please welcome your competitors for the 400m freestyle S11 classification!"

I felt Brian fill in to my right, and I grabbed a hold of his left arm. I could no longer perceive the space around me when we stepped onto the pool deck, as the noise had fully washed out my perception of the world. With eyes that didn't work and ears that were drowned in crowd noise, my only connection to the world was Brian's left arm.

He walked me to a chair with a small basket next to it, and I knew it was time to undress and prepare for the race. Item by item, I pulled off my jacket, my hoodie, and so on until I stood exposed in front of the cheering crowd, clad only in a skin-tight racing suit, my cap, and my goggles. For just a moment, I lost myself amongst the noise. I almost forgot where I was and what I was doing. The world around me seemed so dark and immense that I could barely comprehend it.

Thankfully, Brian took my hand and placed it on the starting block, which snapped me back to the present. The shape and feel of the starting block was so familiar that I didn't have to see it to know what it looked like. I traced out the platform of the block and reached to the front lip. I left my hand there and stretched my mental gaze to the pool in front of me. I didn't need to see the water, the lane lines, the long black line, or the opposing wall to know that they were there. I relied on my memories to conjure a vivid mental image of the pool in front of me.

Nothing else mattered. I was now the one in control of my destiny. I was the only one capable of conquering my own doubts, and proving that while my vision might have been taken away, my spirit couldn't be conquered.

Three blasts of a whistle came from my left as the referee issued the command for silence. In an instant, the screaming fans were quieted, and their cheers were replaced with a silence that seemed to be louder than the cheers from a moment before. Another whistle from the referee beckoned us to step up on the block. I carefully did so and set my feet, with my right toes curled over the front lip and my back foot angled slightly on the fin on the back of the block.

"Take your mark . . ." the referee's voice commanded over a crackled intercom. I bent over, coiled the muscles in my legs and lower back, and gripped the front lip of the block on either side of my right foot.

A buzzer sounded and I unleashed, leaping into the air and arching my back in an attempt to gain as much altitude as possible before gravity inevitably splashed me into the water.

Underwater, I stretched into a long and streamlined position, and undulated my body for four powerful, simultaneous kicks with both legs. I broke out and began setting each hand above my head before pulling through with as much strength and efficiency as I could. At this point, I needed to remind myself not to let my excitement get the best of me. At the beginning of a big race like this one, it's very easy to pop up, spin your wheels, and start burning up valuable energy early in the race.

Brian and I had practiced a certain strategy, and my plan was to keep as much in the tank as possible during the first half of the race. I needed to make every effort to stay long with my stroke, keep control of my breathing, and keep my heart rate as low as possible. This would hopefully keep my pace even, and give me something to work with during the last hundred meters.

I breathed deep on every stroke and cruised through the first length, just grazing the right-hand lane line. Close call, I thought, but I recovered.

Based on an initial study of my competitors, I figured that I should be able to put some distance in between me and the other swimmers, as long as I avoided crashing, of course. To accomplish this, I kept my hands very low on my arm recovery, dragging my fingers across the surface of the water, which helped me feel for the lane line with every stroke. If I found the lane line with either hand, ideally I would be able to correct course in time to prevent bringing my race to a catastrophic halt. While moving at full speed, especially with fatigue setting in, keeping my hands low in this manner often proved very difficult. I would crash frequently in practice.

About a meter from the wall, I received the warning tap on my back from another coach named Andrew. Upon feeling the tap, I kicked my feet over my head in a somersault, planted my feet on the wall, and launched off in the opposite direction. When I made it back to the start side, Brian was there to give me another tap.

Though I could feel my heart rate going up slightly, I felt good all the way through the first half of the race. When I turned at the two hundred meter mark, I made a deliberate effort to begin kicking just a little bit more. I continued to cruise with my arms, but my kick came in powerful bursts: "boom, boom, boom, boom!"

I would quickly rest before another round of "boom, boom, boom, booms!" I worked my way through the fifth length, I felt my arms begin to burn as lactic acid accumulated and fatigue began to set in. I compensated by moving my arms faster and faster, sticking with the bursts of kick.

With two lengths left, I began kicking harder and harder and moving my arms faster and faster, knowing that I was on my last lap and I didn't need to save anything for anybody.

The end of the race went by in a burning flash, and at last, I slammed my left hand into the wall. I picked my head up out of the water to cheers of a magnitude I had never heard before.

Once again, I was lost in the dark. There was no light or sound beyond the static noise of the voluminous crowd. I had no idea what was happening or who had won the gold medal.

I felt like pumping my fist, because I thought that I had executed a great race. But weakened by my recent exertion, doubt found a way to wiggle back into my head. A fist pump would surely look fool-ish if I had lost. What if my efforts hadn't been enough? What if someone in an outside lane just had the race of their life, and that's who the crowd was cheering for?

Without being able to see the scoreboard or hear anyone talking above the continuing crowd noise, I sat alone in the pool in front of eighteen thousand people. I was figuratively drowning amid ev-er-expanding darkness and shadows of doubt. Much like the day in Afghanistan when I saw the mushroom cloud from an IED explo-sion near members of my patrol, those thirty seconds felt like thirty minutes.

Then, the last competitor finished, which prompted the referee to blow his whistle three times, indicating that the race was over. At that point, Brian leaned over and shouted at the top of his lungs, in a distinct voice that I knew so well. He screamed two words that I'll remember forever.

"YOU WON!!!"

The story had come true. One year to the day after losing my eyesight in Afghanistan, I had somehow won the gold medal at the Paralympic Games in London. In that moment, the darkness of being blind was no match for the bright lights of jubilation that suddenly filled my consciousness.

It was the most rewarding moment of my life. September 7, 2012, was my Alive Day, and indeed, I had never felt more alive.

21

Fifty Stars and
Thirteen Stripes

Wearing a Team USA uniform with a large American flag patch on my sleeve, I stood tall at one end of the now serene competition pool. Only a few moments earlier, that same pool had been so alive—so energized—by the finals race and the excited crowd. That same crowd now watched as a delegate from the International Paralympic Committee approached and beckoned me to bow.

The woman slid a large gold medal around my neck and placed a bouquet of flowers in my left hand while shaking my right. She offered her congratulations, and I emphatically thanked her, not making any effort to hide my now-beaming smile.

In front of my family, friends, and eighteen thousand other fans, I proudly threw my hands in the air in a "V," just as I had on the mound at Tropicana Field. The cheers of the crowd were as loud as they had been all night. I smiled even wider, becoming giddy from a flow of emotion and elation that I had only experienced once before:

one year ago to the day, when I thought I was about to be reunited with my departed family members and friends in the afterlife.

I smiled, waved, smiled again, and waved again. The moment seemed to stretch on forever, even if it was only a few minutes. During those few minutes, though, the world, my family, and my community were all saying that they were proud of me, which was all I could have ever hoped for.

The moment came to an abrupt end, however, and the cheering crowd quieted as the sounds of an orchestra filled the arena, heralding the first notes of the "Star-Spangled Banner." I popped to attention, just as I had been taught to do as a young plebe at the US Naval Academy.

As the notes of the anthem played, I was transported back to Dive School, where on the side of a different pool, we put down our SCUBA tanks and fins for a moment while we rendered honors to our country's sacred flag. Afterward, Tyler would lead our class in a booming, "HOOYAH AMERICA" that would echo across the Dive School compound.

As I stood on the podium, I saw Tyler's face—smiling and laughing heartily—which was so powerful that the image will stick with me for the rest of my life. I remembered that same picture projected on a screen during a slideshow at his wake, as hundreds came to pay their respects to Tyler's flag-draped casket. Tyler was such an amazing person and courageous warrior, and he had taught me the power of an incessant positive attitude, and how to look for the good in every person, situation, and circumstance.

I saw Tara's face flash briefly in my mind, and I thought of all the wonderful moments we shared, whether at the Naval Academy, on our getaways, or on the shores of the Chesapeake Bay. I flinched slightly as I was reminded of her suicide and how much I missed her, but it also reminded me how her death had taught me to never take a friendship—or any interaction with another person—for granted.

In Tara's absence, I resolved to wholly invest myself in each of my interpersonal relationships, and to try as hard as I could to be a source of positivity for everyone. I hadn't been able to help Tara, but that didn't mean I couldn't help others. A tear formed at the corner of my eye, but despite the pain of this memory, I was comforted to know that Tara was with me, in some way or another, during this great moment.

My mental gaze drifted to that beautiful, final sunrise amongst the harsh mountains and fertile valleys of Afghanistan. I then remembered laying in the fetal position, staring at little blades of grass as my vision faded away forever. I thought about waiting for my hero—Grandpa Lindsey—to come and take me away for eternity.

I remembered Evan and Leo calling to me, bringing me back to reality, and then helping me to a helicopter. I thought about the pilot and flight crew, all of whom put themselves at great risk to land in a hostile area and transport me to a hospital to receive life-saving medical care. I remembered subsequently being told that it took over twelve hours for a surgeon to put my face back together at the hospital in Kandahar. The surgeon and her entire staff had poured every bit of their hearts into repairing my damaged body.

I remembered being told that I was flown to Germany, where another surgeon and his staff spent hours upon hours putting me back together. Without all of those doctors, surgeons, and nurses, I never would have made it anywhere close to a gold medal podium in England.

I thought of my mom, who had gotten the dreaded phone call about my injury at 5:30 in the morning. The voice on the other end of the phone had informed her that her son had stepped on an IED, and had suffered major wounds to his head and face.

I thought of my brother Mitch, who wrapped his arms around her, and comforted our mom when her entire world was instantly shattered. I thought of my brother Russ, who had shown me what it meant to love someone unconditionally while we were in the hospital in Maryland. I thought of my sister Elyse, who had embraced the broken down, ugly version of Brad, which allowed me to shed expectations and rebuild my self-image.

I thought of my dad and how he had taught me to pursue excellence in everything, and shown me what it meant to be a man of character. I hoped that wherever he was, he was able to witness this moment, and that he would be proud of me.

I thought of my hometown friends and supporters in Florida, who had surrounded me and my family with love and support during our time of adversity. I thought of Lindsay, Jenny, and Fred Lewis, who had offered me the opportunity to show myself and others that blindness wouldn't become an obstacle.

I thought of Rich Cardillo, who had pushed me to consider the Paralympics, and Fred Lambeck, who had initially shown me how. I thought of Guy and Anne Meree, who had presented me with such a golden opportunity, and who had introduced me to my coach, Brian. I thought of Les, who dropped me off for practice every day that summer, then drove us to work afterward. I thought of that crazy morning when Brian and I first realized that I would have the chance to compete for a gold medal on the anniversary of my vision loss. I thought of Brian's excited shouts of "YOU WON!" when the story finally came true.

As trumpets and horns sounded, I thought of a painting I had previously seen of the American flag waving gently in the night sky, which was illuminated by exploding enemy shells during the War of 1812. I thought of the historic Baltimore Harbor, where Francis Scott Key had been inspired to write the "Star-Spangled Banner" while witnessing the very image reflected in the painting, and how moving there had changed my life.

As our flag was hoisted higher than any other in that swimming arena, I came to understand that its fifty stars and thirteen stripes represented so much more than states and colonies. They represented the power of a community. I thought about all those people who had loved me, supported me, taught me, and shared their lives with me, and realized everything that had happened that day was the result of a community's efforts. I would never have made it there if any one of the links in that long chain had not been strong.

My success that day—and the gold medal itself—was not the result of anything I had done as an individual, but as a part of a much wider community. In that moment, I came to understand that individuals never accomplish anything truly great. When communities leverage their cumulative efforts towards a cohesive goal—that is when true greatness can be achieved. The gold medal hanging around my neck belonged to my family, my community, and most of all, my country.

ON NOVEMBER 1, 2013, a group of my closest friends and family gathered in historic Memorial Hall in Annapolis. In that same hall, I had been sworn into service by my uncle, Chuck Allen, in 2002. Later, I served restriction in that hall as punishment for being a lazy midshipman. It was also inside Memorial Hall where I had first stared at the miniature John Ripley and up at Oliver Hazard Perry's battle flag, and resolved to be a leader of character and to serve in combat.

Nearly a decade later, my family gathered to help me bring that short legacy to a close, as I was about to retire from naval service. At some point between my injury and the fall of 2013, and to this day I am unclear as to how, the administrative separation process that had been initiated by the Navy as a result of my DUI was dropped. This allowed me to instead medically retire with honors, for which I will always be grateful. The brawny EOD warfare officer that had sat across from me during that selection interview so many years ago, now a two-star admiral, proceeded to pin one last piece of flare onto my uniform before guiding me to a podium.

For my family and the civilians in the room, I shared some of the history that makes Memorial Hall so special, and more specifically, why it is so special to me. The small crowd erupted in laughter as I recalled the "two left shoes" incident, and then listened intently as I recalled being on that southern Afghanistan mountaintop with Sarge on the night that Osama bin Laden was killed. I reflected on how in that moment, I truly understood and felt connected to my purpose, which was to serve.

I reflected on the journey that had gotten me to that point, beginning in Weeki Wachee Springs, near the home of my Grandpa Lindsey. I told the story of my grandpa's heroism, and how he had been a true representative of what has been called the "Greatest Generation" by many. I recalled how from a very early age, I wanted to follow in my grandfather's footsteps, as many in my generation have resolved to do. In our efforts, some, including the commander-in-chief, have come to refer to us as the "Next Greatest Generation."

Standing in Memorial Hall, whose walls are decorated with battle flags from every conflict since the Revolutionary War, I proposed that there is no such thing as a "Greatest Generation." Instead, I explained my belief that greatness can be found in every generation. There will always be those who are willing to lay down their lives in the name of liberty; to commit to a life of service in order to work toward a better world for their family and future generations.

Our founding fathers first stitched together the red, white, and blue to represent a New World predicated on freedom, tolerance, and equal opportunity. Since then, our flag has been the guiding light for our countrymen, throughout our great nation's growth and development, and through our bouts with civil war, foreign dictators, fascism, cold war, and our current war on terror. Challenge has always been a way of life for our country, and therefore, should be a way of life for each and every one of us.

From the example of our forefathers and the teachings of my dad, coupled with my experiences on the battlefield and the field of competition, I learned the value of virtue and the composition of character. I came to believe that by pursuing excellence and virtue in all aspects of life, we may all become persons of character, and be empowered to fully enjoy our freedom. To me, that is what it means to be an American.

It pained me to leave the ranks of the Navy in 2013, but I left with the resolution that my commitment to serve would not end with my official naval service. I was—and will always be—deeply honored to have been a part of that tradition, and to have served with the best and brightest men and women in the world.

My commitment to my family, my country, and our flag is forever. Through bloodshed on the battlefield, I will always be a part of those fifty stars and thirteen stripes, which serve as my guiding light.

To this day, the light burns deep within me. It is a fire in my eyes that will never be extinguished.

AFTERWORD

The Delta

I listened intently as a small car—probably a four-cylinder Honda Civic or something like it—came to a halt in front of me, just to my left. From behind me and to my right, a much larger vehicle—some sort of truck or SUV, perhaps—revved its engine and passed along my right side.

Surmising that the light had changed, I commanded my new guide dog, Gizzy, to move forward. The beautiful, seventy-five pound, long-haired German Shepherd followed my command exactly before weaving us around the Honda Civic, which had pulled just a little too far into the crosswalk.

Gizzy slowed as we approached the opposing curb, which prompted me to feel around in front with my foot.

"Forward!" I once again commanded her after finding the curb's lip.

Gizzy moved in exactly the right way, which prevented me from stubbing my toe and potentially tripping on the low curb.

"Good girl," I said.

The sounds of traffic faded behind us as we walked deeper into Baltimore's Patterson Park, a vast community park just north of my new row home on the harbor. I felt Gizzy tense with excitement and pull a little harder as she recognized the path to the large, fenced-in dog park, which perhaps should be called "Patterson Bark."

Gizzy's wagging tail beat at the back of my left leg as she guided me to the gate of the park. I opened it, and then followed the chain link fence to my right to a park bench. After unclipping Gizzy's leash, I removed her harness and commanded her by saying "down," and then "stay." Gizzy obeyed, and then patiently watched as I folded up her gear and settled on the park bench.

I pictured Gizzy's stare intensifying as I removed a tennis ball from my jacket pocket. It was a chilly morning—the first really chilly morning since the summer heat abated—so there were no other people or dogs in the park, to the best of my knowledge. I chucked the ball to the opposite side of the park.

Gizzy's dog tags jingled as her gaze undoubtedly followed the ball, but still, she obediently remained where she lay.

"Free!" I commanded, which sent Gizzy running to fetch the tennis ball.

The wind picked up, sending a chill down my spine. I zipped my jacket all the way up, and then jammed my hands even further into my pockets. I listened to Gizzy's tags jingling as she ran back and forth across the park, happily chewing on her favorite tennis ball.

As a Florida boy, I have always felt distaste for the cold, but Gizzy, with her long coat of fur, seemed to perk up when the mercury dropped. She occasionally brought the ball back, while beckoning me to toss the progressively more and more slobbery ball across the park. Mostly, though, she kept to herself, and was just content to walk around gnawing on the ball.

After a while, I started feeling the cold really set in, and decided that it was time to head home. I whistled for Gizzy to come back so

I could put her gear back on and we'd be on our way. The only problem was that Gizzy had other plans.

I heard Gizzy's tags jingle back and forth in front of me—just out of my reach—as she indicated to me that she wasn't ready to leave the park yet. At first, I chuckled at this display of independence, but as the game went on, my fingers and toes became more numb. I got progressively more annoyed by the cold and Gizzy's reluctance to leave, and all of a sudden, the game wasn't funny anymore.

"Let's go!" I barked.

Despite probably sensing my voice's growing strain, Gizzy started running circles around me. She was just out of my reach and pleasantly ignorant of the distress this game was causing me.

My frustration gave way to desperation, and then helplessness. Here I was, an almost thirty-year-old man who was wholly dependent on a two-year-old puppy. The dog had complete control over the current situation, while I had absolutely none.

If Gizzy wouldn't come back, what was I supposed to do? I could have found my way back to the gate, but then what? I was a quarter mile deep inside a giant park. I might have been able to feel my way back to that busy intersection, but could I have subsequently crossed the street without the help of a dog or my cane? Along with the cold weather, the thought of large trucks buzzing by as I felt my way around like a mummy made me shudder.

"Get back over here!" I growled at Gizzy.

She only ran around faster, though, and seemed to thoroughly enjoy this childish game of tag, which I was losing terribly.

A feeling of almost overwhelming panic set in. My heart rate elevated, and my frustration clouded my ability to think through and work out a solution to this problem. Here I was: a former bomb technician and current Paralympic athlete, whose steel nerves had allowed me to succeed in some of the most difficult situations in the world. Now, I was completely helpless in a dog park, despite being only a mile from my house.

Had I not been so frustrated, I probably would have laughed, but the thoughts racing through my head only made me more upset. I sat back on the park bench, held my head in my hands and focused on my breathing, in order to let the frustration subside. There was nothing I could do about this at this particular point, so I needed to simply let it go. Once I relaxed, my heart rate returned to normal, and the cloud of frustration in my head began to subside.

Moments like this one actually occurred relatively often in the few years following the Paralympics. I would get completely turned around and lost, for instance, in the alley behind my house while trying to take out the garbage. I made a horrible mess when I was first learning how to pick up after Gizzy's bathroom breaks. I broke a lot of plates and glasses while cleaning up the kitchen. I smacked my head on open cupboard doors, lamp posts, and low-hanging tree branches.

The Internet wouldn't always play nice with my computer's screen reader, so simple tasks like ordering dog food or paying the electric bill became prohibitively difficult, if not impossible. I would then spend hours on the phone, working my way through an endless labyrinth of automated menu systems trying to accomplish those same simple tasks. Each time I hit a wall, literally or figuratively, I would get flustered in the same manner. Like that day in the dog park, the helplessness I frequently faced in the simplest of situations would sometimes frustrate me to the point of panic.

Over time, the frequency of these situations began to decrease. I would either find ways around a given problem, or ways to avoid it altogether. For example, I started going to the dog park only when I knew that other people would be there. I set up auto pay for every possible bill. I started using the Amazon app on my iPhone to order coffee and dog food, and by doing so, streamlined my way through tricky web pages that may or may not be accessible to the blind. More importantly than bills or dog food, though, I found the source of my underlying issue.

While doing an interview for a 2015 article that appeared in *The Players' Tribune*, I was attempting to describe this phenomenon; how sometimes the most frustrating aspects of my blindness can be found in the simplest of tasks. In my description, it dawned on me that my frustration in each of these situations was not from the task or the situation itself, but from the comparison of this task or situation to how it would have been before I lost my vision.

Washing dishes did not used to be a struggle for me. It was an absolutely mindless task, much like mopping a floor or vacuuming a carpet. Without my vision, though, washing dishes became like walking through a minefield, which I had some experience with.

The first time I tried to wash the dishes since becoming blind, I had to very carefully feel my way through several precariously arranged stacks of dirty plates, and then load them into an equally disorganized dishwasher before hand-washing the delicate items. The delicates then needed to be loaded onto a dish rack that may or may not already have contained other glasses, plates, or bowls somewhere on the edge.

Much like disabling an IED, one false move during this process would result in an explosion, only this time made of ceramics and glass. After I screwed up, my mess became a hundred times more difficult to clean, and much more dangerous since little shards of glass were everywhere. Not only were my feet at risk, but what about poor Gizzy, who immediately came running into the kitchen to see if I was okay?

"Out of here!" I yelled while bending down to start picking out the biggest pieces.

I then started fumbling around under the sink in an effort to find a dustpan that was probably not even there. My frustration mounted even further when I realized that it was somewhere in the basement.

"This used to be so freaking easy," I said to myself.

But that's just it. If I had grown up my entire life washing dishes in the dark, I would have learned how to take my time, carefully work my way through the dirty dishes, and neatly organize the dishwasher a certain way before checking the dry rack for dishes before loading it up again. It would take me a little longer than most other people, but so what?

It wasn't the task of washing dishes that I initially found so frustrating, it was the difference between how it used to be and how it is now. I began to call this difference, which for so long served as the root cause of my frustration, "the delta." The more I focused on "the delta" between how life used to be and how it is now, the more I got frustrated.

After identifying "the delta," my entire perspective began to change. So what if it now took me a while to order dog food or pay the electric bill by phone? That's just how it is now, I thought, and there is no sense in comparing it to anything else.

As this light bulb went on in my head, I started to think over different situations in the past where I might have gotten frustrated. Whether it was sitting in traffic, the latest episode of my favorite TV show being accidentally deleted from the DVR, or waiting in line at the airport or grocery store, all were situations where frustration had arisen out of a mismatch of expectations.

This mismatch in expectations is exactly what I mean by "the delta." It's always a difference between where you are, who you are, what your situation is, and where you wish you were, who you want to be, or what situation you'd rather find yourself in.

It took the experience of being blown up in Afghanistan and subsequently living life as a blind man to realize that if we can find ways to minimize "the delta"—to minimize the mismatch in our expectations—then it will allow us to exist in a given moment and appreciate it for what it is, rather than what we wish it was. I'll spare you the cliché about wishing into a cup and seeing how fast it fills up, but let's just say that I've learned not to put a lot of stock in wishes. I hiked through a number of deserts, but never found any lamps or genies.

In combat, we used a tactic called threat assessment, which takes into account all the different variables in your current situation. It then identifies each "threat" and subsequently ranks each of those from highest to lowest. You then address each threat individually; one after another.

If there was an IED right in front of me, for instance, it didn't matter that there was a Taliban fighter shooting at me from three hundred yards away. Both are threats, but the IED is a greater one in that specific moment. After I addressed the IED, I could then confront the Taliban fighter. It would have done me no good to try to address both at the same time. By dividing my focus, I would have impeded my overall ability to negotiate each threat. When the stakes are life or death, I would of course always want to be fully engaged as I addressed each threat.

I came to believe that threat assessment is immediately relevant to everyday life. Sure, the stakes are much different, but in any given situation, there are hundreds of variables at play. If you take a moment to work through these variables, you can easily sort them into two distinct categories: things you can control or influence, and things that you can't.

You can't control the things you can't control, so it's worthless to worry about them. Things like the weather, traffic patterns, and the gas are variables that probably affect your day-to-day existence, but you can't control them, so it behooves you to accept them for what they are. On the flip side, if you sort out the things you can control, the list is much shorter. Like in threat assessment, if you rank these variables from most important to least, you can then attack each variable with your full focus. As you negotiate each "threat," you just work your way down the list.

By learning to accept each situation for what it is, dismissing the variables you can't control, and leveraging your full focus to each of the variables you can influence, you have optimized your role in that particular moment. Over time, if you can establish a habit involving those tactics, you can optimize your effect on your own fate or destiny.

You cannot control who you used to be. History is just that: history. Of course, history is a wonderful resource, as it may inform us about what to expect in the future. But history doesn't always drive the current moment.

The same is true for the future. We cannot control it, and try as we might to predict it, we're almost always wrong. That being said, I now believe that comparing your current situation to another in the past, or dismissing your current situation by dreaming of a different set of circumstances sometime in the distant future, is effectively a fruitless, wasted endeavor.

Instead, I believe that the most prudent thing we can do is to accept every situation and every set of circumstances for what they are. In doing so, you can then evaluate every variable in your set of circumstances individually: dismissing the variables you can't control, and deciding to vector your complete focus to the variables that you can influence. I believe that by doing this, you can tackle nearly any situation, while effectively managing its associated stresses.

Going one step further, I believe this "delta" concept can apply on a macro level as well. One of the reasons that 2012 was such a remarkable year for me and my family was how rapidly we were able to make such a significant transition. In a single year, I went from being a deployed service member, serving as a subject matter expert in explosive hazard mitigation, to being a member of Team USA, where I would serve as a blind swimmer who joined the ranks of champions.

Along with the change in vocation came an equal, if not a more rapid and significant, change in my self-perception. In losing my vision, I lost a lot of capability, which was so clearly illustrated for me on the day that I chased Gizzy around the dog park, or when I smashed those plates in the kitchen. Succeeding in the Paralympic realm went a long way toward filling that void, but it still took a long while afterward to fully adjust. It took me a while to rebuild my self-perception, and mitigate that difference—"the delta"—in my own mind.

It was identifying this "delta" as the core component of my struggle that allowed me to understand, and then mitigate, the negative effect it had on my self-perception. I came to understand that I could no longer live in the shadow of who I used to be. I used to be Brad Snyder, EOD warfare officer. That Brad has transformed into who I am now, Brad Snyder, US Paralympian. We can define ourselves in an infinite amount of ways, but that definition is up to us. I had to make a conscious decision to leave behind the person I was, and to become the person that I am.

In Eric Greitens's *Resilience*, the former Navy SEAL challenges the traditional definition of his own book's title. "Resilience" has traditionally been defined as the ability of a substance or object to "spring back" to its original form. Over the past few years, for instance, a lot of people have congratulated me on my "resilience," and told me how impressed they were that I was able to "bounce back." While I appreciated their sentiments, those comments just didn't jibe with me for some reason.

The reason finally clicked when I read Greitens's alternative definition of resilience as a non-elastic term. Instead of the substance or object "springing back" to its original form, perhaps resilience means that the substance or object can thrive in any set of circumstances, or any situation. My success in the Paralympics is not an example of how I "sprung back" to my original form. That's because there is no such thing as an original form.

Each of us is a dynamic entity; a function of our life's experiences. We are an aggregate of everything we have seen, heard, tasted, and felt. Each new moment presents a wealth of opportunity to learn and grow, and in each moment, we are a different form than we were in the previous moment.

I transformed. I had to accept a new set of circumstances, and resolve to thrive anyway. That is what "resilience" means to me. It is the resolution to thrive, no matter what. "Don't give up the ship."

Living in the shadow of your former self is potentially as damaging as living in the shadow of who you want to be. So many of us get wrapped up in where we're going, we forget both where and who we are. When I was younger, I wanted so badly to gain acceptance into the Naval Academy. Once I was there, I wanted to earn my place in the Special Operations community. Once there, I wanted to serve in combat, and so on and so forth. I spent nearly eleven years trying to become something different than what I was.

Don't get me wrong, I admire ambition, and I think goal-setting is a critically important tool in attaining eventual success. But it's just that: a tool. I think it's just as important not to define yourself by your goals or ambitions, but to learn to accept—and be happy with—who you are.

As of this writing, I have goals and ambitions to again be part of Team USA in Rio de Janeiro, Brazil, for the 2016 Paralympic Games. I hope to start a company one day, and eventually a family as well. These goals and ambitions inform my future, and drive me in certain directions, but I no longer define myself by who I want to become. Instead, I am happy to just be Brad Snyder.

Needless to say, I have learned a lot in thirty or so years, but the most important lessons have all proven their value in the trying times I experienced between 2009 and 2011. In that short span, I experienced a great deal of loss, but from those experiences, I believe that I also gained a great deal of wisdom. My dad taught me the value of pursuing excellence in every endeavor, and I have seen its virtue come to fruition in multiple arenas. I have also come to understand the power of an optimistic outlook.

I believe that each of us—including the blind—sees the world we want to see. If you make a conscious decision to look for the positive in every situation, that's almost always what you will encounter. I have come to understand the importance of interpersonal relationships, while also learning to never take them for granted.

In any given day, we probably interact with a hundred people. Sometimes more, sometimes less. After these interactions, I ask myself: were my interactions with each of those people something they'll remember as positive or negative?

Did I enrich those people's lives somehow, or did I say something that was upsetting?

Did I treat each of those people with the dignity and respect that I want to be treated with?

One thing I have definitely learned is that you never know what could happen when you take your next step. Therefore, it's absolutely critical to make the most of every moment. If you refuse to allow your existence to be overshadowed by the past—or future—every minute of your life can be magical.

SEATED ON A PARK bench during that same chilly morning in the heart of "Patterson Bark," I perked up when I heard the jingle of the gate. I listened intently as a friendly sounding young woman brought her own dog into the park. She cheerfully tossed a ball for her dog, then came and sat next to me. After a minute or two of small talk, she made a generous offer to help me corral Gizzy, which I gratefully accepted.

As I knelt down to clip on Gizzy's leash, my guide dog licked my face and thanked me for the trip to the dog park. Indeed, Gizzy simply thought the whole "not wanting to leave the park" thing was just a thoroughly enjoyable game, and was totally oblivious to my distress. Back in control of the situation and my frustration completely cleared, I bid farewell to my cheery passerby savior before beginning the trek back home.

Blind or not, I believe that we all have these types of moments. We all get lost, stumble, and sometimes fall, but eventually, we get back up.

Sure, I have been lost in the dark in back alleys, airports, and occasionally my own house, but me still being here today is a testament to one fact that I can affirm as one hundred percent true. We will all eventually find our way.

ACKNOWLEDGMENTS:
BRAD SNYDER

It would be impossible to adequately thank all of the people to whom I owe acknowledgments for enabling me to become the person I am, but here is my best attempt.

First, I must thank my mother, my brothers, and my lovely sister for being there for me all my life, but especially in the trying times outlined in this book. Through everything, the most important thing I have learned is that I am truly lucky to have such an amazing family, and I am forever grateful for their company and counsel, let alone their unfaltering love and support. I would also like to thank my dad for imbuing in me such a strong sense of virtue, and I can only hope that he's proud of the man I have become.

I owe my life to Adam and all the handsome devils I deployed with to Afghanistan. Thank you for the best (and worst) year I have experienced. Thanks to my EOD platoon for standing with me during such a crazy time. Thank you to all those who have offered their lives to protect our liberty—especially Tyler—and those I had the pleasure and honor of serving with during my relatively brief naval career. Special thanks to the boys on my first platoon, whose patient guidance and instruction set me on a straight path.

Tara, I thank you for challenging me to understand the true depth of the word "love." I don't know that I'll ever love anyone the way I loved you, but you have taught me how to truly invest myself in someone else. Thanks to Michael for helping me to remember Tara, and to fully understand and appreciate the impact she had on all of us.

I would like to thank all past, present, and future members of the NMSD brotherhood for allowing me to be a part of the tradition of excellence.

Special thanks to Ian, Pete, Nick, Jake, Sean, Christian, Andy and Caroline, Ryan and Meg, and Rob and Ali for being amazing people and even better friends. I can't believe I am so lucky to have people like you in my life.

I wish I could name the hospital personnel and caretakers who were responsible for helping me and my family while I was hurt, but as you know from reading this book, I was pretty out of it at the time. I hope all of you know how eternally grateful I am for what you did for me, and for all of the other wounded service members who left parts of themselves in Afghanistan and Iraq. Special thanks to Katherine, Lindsay, Lauren, and Ron for fixing me and challenging me to not only return to "normal," but to become better than I was in the first place.

Thanks to Fred, Fred, Rich, and Brian for introducing me to the Paralympics, and for giving me the spark I needed. Thanks to Guy, Anne Meree, and Les for giving me an opportunity to prove my resilience.

Thanks to my Uncle Chuck for not only being a constant mentor over the last sixteen years or so, but also for connecting me with Tom. Finally, thanks to Tom and the folks at Da Capo Press for believing that this story was worth telling. Without them, *Fire in My Eyes* would never have happened.

ACKNOWLEDGMENTS:
TOM SILEO

After finishing *Brothers Forever*, I spent several subsequent months brainstorming a second book project with my wonderful agent, E. J. McCarthy, and my trusted editor, Robert Pigeon. Despite some strong leads, we still hadn't been able to find that brilliant, special idea in the spring of 2015.

During one particular phone call with E. J., I got an e-mail from one of my oldest friends, Brad Allen. I had known Brad since third grade, when we were both growing up just outside our nation's capital in Vienna, Virginia.

After that spring 2015 phone call with my agent, I replied to Brad Allen's e-mail, which contained a video link to an inspiring story about another Brad, who was an Iraq and Afghanistan war veteran and Paralympic gold medalist. As I would soon learn, Brad Snyder was also the nephew of Brad Allen's father, Chuck Allen.

"Uncle Chuck" subsequently put Brad Snyder and me in touch. I want to take this opportunity to sincerely thank you, Chuck, for not only your dedicated service to our country, but for your instrumental contribution in helping make *Fire in My Eyes* a reality.

During my first phone call with Brad Snyder, I instantly knew that he was a real-life American hero with an incredible story to tell. Working with this wounded veteran and Paralympic champion has been the best experience of my career, and I hope you—the reader—are as inspired by Brad's courage as I am. Thank you, Brad, for allowing me to help you make this book the best that it could be. Your remarkable story of sacrifice is a testament to the courage of America's veterans.

I am eternally thankful for the counsel and friendship of the best literary agent in the world, E. J. McCarthy, for seeing the potential in not only *Fire in My Eyes* and *Brothers Forever*, and but in me as an author. It has been equally thrilling to work with Robert Pigeon, Lissa Warren, Kevin Hanover, Sean Maher, and the entire Da Capo Press/ Perseus Books Group team on a second project. I feel truly blessed to be learning from the best people in the publishing business.

Thank you to my wife, Lisa, for your patience, hard work, and unconditional love, to which I owe my entire career as an author. Thank you to our young daughter, Reagan, for lighting up our lives. Thank you to my mom, Diane, and my dad, Dr. Bob, for making sure that I grew up with a good education, strong family, and appreciation of life.

Thank you to my grandparents, Canio, Hedy, Clarence, and Betty, for all that you sacrificed during World War II. You taught me what it means to be an American.

Thank you to all US service members, veterans, and military family members—especially those who have lost a loved one—who have trusted me to help tell your stories in book and column form. You are the real-life American heroes that my daughter will grow up learning about.

Finally, thank you to Brad Allen for your enduring friendship. This once in a lifetime opportunity to work on *Fire in My Eyes* would never have come to fruition without you. Most importantly, thank you for helping me make another great friend named Brad.

INDEX